Not to Scale

How the
Small
Becomes
Large,
the Large Becomes
Unthinkable,
and the Unthinkable Becomes
Possible

———

Jamer Hunt

GRAND CENTRAL
PUBLISHING

NEW YORK   BOSTON

Grand Central Publishing
Hachette Book Group
1290 Avenue of the Americas, New York, NY 10104
grandcentralpublishing.com
twitter.com/grandcentralpub

First Edition: March 2020

Grand Central Publishing is a division of Hachette Book Group, Inc. The Grand Central Publishing name and logo is a trademark of Hachette Book Group, Inc.

The publisher is not responsible for websites (or their content) that are not owned by the publisher.

The Hachette Speakers Bureau provides a wide range of authors for speaking events. To find out more, go to www.hachettespeakersbureau.com or call (866) 376-6591.

Library of Congress Cataloging-in-Publication Data has been applied for.

ISBNs: 978-1-5387-1588-8 (hardcover), 978-1-5387-5134-3 (international trade), 978-1-5387-1-5895 (ebook)

Printed in the United States of America

LSC-C

10 9 8 7 6 5 4 3 2 1

To Cynthia Holt Hunt

Contents

Introduction   How Much Does a Gigabyte Weigh?   1

Chapter 01   On Exactitude in Science   23

Chapter 02   The Figure and the Ground   45

Chapter 03   These Go to 11   67

Chapter 04   Tiny Violence   101

Chapter 05   The Numb of Numbers   123

Chapter 06   Scalar Framing   139

Chapter 07   The Middle   173

Chapter 08   Feral Pigs and Wicked Problems   201

Chapter 09   Presence   223

Acknowledgments   233

Notes   237

Index   247

About the Author   261

Not to
Scale

How Much Does a Gigabyte Weigh?

Bubble levels and outdoor thermometers. Compasses and alarm clocks. We used to make these in factories and keep them in our toolboxes and on our bedside tables. Today, they are "utilities," bundled for free on our smartphones, just a thumb swipe and a finger tap away. As children, we cobbled together compasses from a piece of cork, a sewing needle, and a magnet; or built a sundial clock from sticks and stones. Comprised of microcircuits, electrons, lines of code, and glowing pixels, the compass and watch in our smartphones might as well have been made by tiny elves using pixie dust. The disappearance of these mechanical tools into the inner workings of the smartphone is a transformation barely short of magic. Few of us would know how, let alone dare, to tinker with the compass in our phone. Where would we even find it...whatever *it* is?

In some significant way each of these instruments—the

level, the thermometer, the compass, and the clock—also helps us to navigate scale. Each organizes invisible forces—orientation, temperature, direction, and time—into perceptible ones. From sensation comes measurement; from chaos comes order. The bubble, or spirit, level plumbs surfaces, situating us in the universe. The physics of its operation is utterly self-evident: A bubble of air trapped in a glass tube filled with colored ethanol (the spirit) lists left or right, up or down, depending on the levelness of the surface. When the bubble comes to rest evenly between the machine-inscribed marks, or scale, things are level, or plumb. A thermometer is similarly straightforward: A small, sealed, glass tube is filled with a dab of mercury. Mercury, being sensitive to temperature, expands as it warms up and contracts as it cools. Once the tube is oriented vertically, the mercury rises as the temperature rises and falls as it falls. Graduated markings add relative degrees of quantitative precision, helping us to decide whether it's a day for a light sweater or a heavier coat. In ways that were casually reassuring, the level, thermometer, compass, and alarm clock all evidenced their mechanics. We could relate to their operation. They each interacted with a seemingly ungovernable set of forces and made them knowable.

By turning these tools into functions, and by embedding them deep into the guts of a smartphone, engineers and designers transformed a relatively dumb object, the cellular phone, into a multifunction Swiss Army knife on steroids. As of 2019 Apple's App Store was home to more than two million

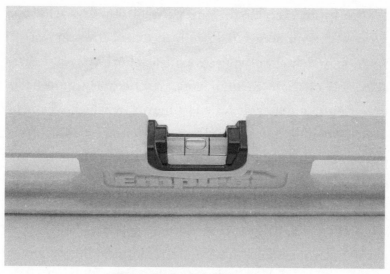

Fig. 1. *Traditional bubble level.*

apps—that's two million different configurations of functions that one's smartphone could deliver. This dematerialization of knowable, physical things into infinitesimal, glowing pixels has transformed not only our economies and lives over the past half century but has also remade our perceptual universe. And where people such as travel agents, traffic reporters, and even friends used to provide services to us on the sidewalks and in the storefronts of our communities, they now more likely exist as complex algorithms somewhere within the apps on our smartphones. As we have drifted from a geographically bounded economy based on hard goods and real people to a networked, global one fueled by information, services, software, and artificial intelligence, we are losing touch, quite literally, with the scale of the known world.

We spend exceedingly long parts of our days with our eyes and ears immersed in digitally mediated environments— working, watching, playing, relaxing—but the physical characteristics of those environments are effectively unrelatable to our human senses. If scale is a means by which we orient ourselves within our environmental surroundings, what happens to us when we cannot touch, smell, taste, hear, or even see their operation? *Not to Scale* is an X-ray of our present cultural moment. Rooted in the fields of design, technology, and culture, we will bound across science, politics, photography, anthropology, systems thinking, and business innovation in order to demonstrate the pervasive, distorting effects of subtle scalar shifts. Scale is not simply a way to measure the size of things around us. It is a formidable conceptual framework. We shape scale, but scale also shapes us ... though we scarcely pay heed to it. Thinking and acting *through* scale, in all of its strange complexity, may be our best strategy for thriving in a dynamically changing world.

Few things should be more self-evident than scale, but it can be one of those concepts that gets more befuddling the longer one stares at it. We usually think of it, in its simplest sense, as a way to assess how big or small things are. The *Cambridge Dictionary* defines *scale* as "a range of numbers used as a system to measure or compare things." For many, scale is nothing more than a tool for organizing information and collecting facts: Musicians understand scale as a particular scaffold of notes; urban planners use scale to distinguish

Fig. 2. *Digital level.*

geographical subunits; and businesses view scale as a means to measure productivity or sales. And the flexibility of the concept of scale allows it to work as effectively for physical properties (length, mass, temperature) as it does for less precisely measurable things (headaches and crushes).

Through scale we can grasp the invisible: Calendars and clocks locate us across a continuum of astronomical or circadian cycles, marking months and hours and minutes and seconds. Maps and compasses locate us in space. This instrumentation of scale has become so hardwired into our perception that we now feel as though linear time, calendrical dates, and cardinal directions are a natural part of the physical world. In reality, scale is merely a human construct that we layer on top of the things we encounter so that our experiences make greater sense.

A recent scan of my laptop's hard drive revealed that it holds more than 1,800,000 files. I have no idea what most of these are, or how I accumulated them. It was only a few years ago that I learned what a gigabyte was, and now my hard drive is hurtling toward one terabyte. My laptop holds tens of thousands of family photos, home movies, mortgage and passport applications, music, book manuscripts, passwords, marked-up e-books, health records, its own applications and operating systems, and who knows what else. The numbers just keep climbing.

One upside of this is that work from the last twenty years of my life no longer clogs up space and accumulates dust in our basement. Orderly rows of nested file icons have replaced moldering cardboard boxes as physical matter has dematerialized into ones and zeroes...ons and offs. All of that work is now always available and at my fingertips, built no longer upon diverse arrangements of atoms and molecules but upon a shared substrate of electrons and code. And it is all shoehorned into a machine so thin that it can slide effortlessly into a manila envelope. Miraculously—and paradoxically—at this very same moment that the digital footprint of my data-life is swelling uncontrollably, the size of my laptop is, improbably, shrinking. Each new iteration of my laptop both holds more and is smaller. More is begetting more and yet, somehow, more is also becoming less. Size and scale have become unmoored from how we experience things.

These transformations are more than just technological innovations. They raise unexpected, existential questions. For instance, the entirety of my work life and much of my personal history exists in a form that I can no longer see or hold in my hand. I'm haunted by the fact that I cannot touch it and I cannot see it. My digital life could evaporate in a flash, or a crash. What would the loss of all that mean to who I am? For almost all of human existence, until very recently, we could easily size up the things that made up our work and personal life—we could fathom the size of our file cabinets with our eyes, lift them to gauge their weight, smell the musty stacks of old papers for a clue to their age. Today, a significant part of my identity now floats about in a digital ether to which I have little perceptual access. In some strange way these circuits and electrons have shaped who I am and become part of my every experience. How much, I wonder, does a gigabyte even weigh?

A modern, digital process as seemingly straightforward as email—type out a message and hit Send and it rockets down a pipe to its destination inbox—actually obeys a logic that defies commonsense understanding. The protocol of packet switching by which an email arrives at its destination—the slicing of a sent email into tiny parts, scattered to the winds of multiple internet servers, ricocheting around the globe, and then reassembled at the other end—is just one instance of the numberless ways in which relatively easy-to-understand communication services have outstripped the operational imagination of most simple humans. This is a far cry from lashing a message to a pigeon's leg.

And a recent *Chronicle Review* headline provocatively asked, "Is Email Making Professors Stupid?"[1] Three decades into the launch of commercial email services and we are struggling with the effects that this digital transformation has wrought. Just as storytelling and acting changed with the shift from the visual scale of movies to that of television, the way we communicate also changed in the evolution of stamped mail to electronic mail. It's not uncommon today for a working professional to receive more than one hundred emails a day, something that never would have occurred with physical mail. The shift in medium has spawned new behaviors (overzealous cc'ing, never-ending conversation threads, spam) so that we are now so awash in it that we must ask if it's actually making us dumber. A shift in scale—to weightless and seemingly cost free—has created a cascading shift in social behaviors and an increasing awareness that the medium is killing our capacity to focus and get work done.

If the oddities of scale lived only within the inner workings of laptops and computers, we could dismiss them as technological eccentricities. But the quandaries of my laptop are just one symptom of a tectonic shift in scale that many of us experience—but most of us do not see. More significant, we encounter these disruptions in matters of much vaster social import than our laptops' storage and our email frustrations.

———

Not to Scale explores our place within unpredictable systems, the forces reshaping them, and our anxious uncertainty in interacting with them. We yearn to know how our puny, individual actions can lead to more positive impacts, but the problem is that simple cause-and-effect thinking is constantly upended by the aftershocks of scalar change. Through our human endeavors we push scales: We make things bigger, faster, stronger, tinier, heavier, or even more complex. But we must also realize that scale pushes back. Its behaviors are often unruly and its effects immeasurable. The phenomena these scales unleash can break instruments, unsettle our sense of self, and confound our ability to navigate complex issues.

"Paper or plastic?" Perhaps no question more quintessentially embodies our modern quandary. We usually encounter this simple question when we're checking out at the supermarket, just aiming to get home to make a Tuesday night dinner. But it freezes us in our tracks: An insignificant choice telescopes out into a tangle of unexpected issues. Will our decision in that innocuous moment lead to more felled trees, the loss of carbon sequestering, the decline of natural cooling processes, and to increased transportation costs? Or will it perpetuate the production of a poisonous, nonrenewable, fossil fuel product that will live in landfills for more generations than we can count? Every question leads to yet another one, and the fate of our planet seems to hang in the balance. What might have been in simpler times a decision of convenience or preference has evolved instead into an intractable moral quandary at a global scale. I thought I had the dilemma figured out: I started to bring my own canvas bags. Hah...problem solved! That was until I discovered that many of the reusable grocery tote bags we buy are made in China using an energy-intensive process that includes hazardous, lead-based printing materials. Not only do these manufacturing practices contaminate groundwater at the site of production, but the lead printing can also leach into the food in the bags themselves.[2] So much for my clever reframing.

Paper or plastic? Own or lease? Shop local or buy online? Fly or Skype? Public or private? Sustainable or convenient? Fast or slow? Recycle or reuse? Each of these daily dilemmas—small in the scope of our personal lives—expands enormously in import when weighed against their wider role in putting at risk our social, environmental, and technological futures. Unexpected changes in scale have disrupted cause and effect and our capacity to understand how things work. They have remapped the relationship between our conception of the world (the mind) and our perception of it (the body). Challenges that we used to be able to resolve using strategies, tools, knowledge, and help from the people around us no longer respond in quite the same way. More than that, it has become harder and harder to draw boundaries around the actual problems themselves.

For instance, if we want to help to improve our local

public schools, do we look to the classroom (the books, the desks, the lighting, the schedule, the curriculum) or to the teachers? Given the massive underfunding of school districts in many urban centers, perhaps we should start at the scale of the school districts themselves, or the local, state, or national politicians who systematically underfund these districts? Or to the unions? Or the tax laws that provide the revenue? But maybe, as some experts have pointed out, we won't see any improvement in the performance of children from under-served communities until the social and economic prospects of their neighborhoods improve? Or until we overcome deeply systemic racism? Or improve our public schools? Where do we even start... given that so many have tried and failed already? How can we better our schools when we can hardly design our way out of a paper bag? Simply determining at which scale to act is making "wicked problems" like these even more unsolvable. Should concerned parents, for instance, address the problem by starting at the scale of the students, or the classroom, or the school, or the school system, or the local, state, or national government? Factors and actors at each level seem to contribute to the mess. And should the starting point be different for a teacher? Or a politician?

A relatively narrow problem now instantly ricochets in all directions at once. What we might have once been able to address at the local level is now a massive entanglement in scope and scale. This condition is not entirely new: For decades experts have instructed us to think globally but act locally in order to manage this chaos. But this assumes that thinking "globally" is necessarily a straightforward endeavor. What happens when thinking globally itself becomes so complex and unwieldy that it makes every problem seem hopelessly snarled and out of scale?

It would be nice to believe that we can simply design, plan, and act ourselves out of the most vexing problems of our time, but the evidence for that is scant. Despite decades of damning discoveries, for instance, we have collectively managed only meager responses to what is a clear, imminent, and incontrovertible global climate catastrophe. Similarly, the public school system in economically disadvantaged neighborhoods in the United States (the wealthiest country in the world by GDP) is in such disarray that the influx of $100 million from Facebook founder Mark Zuckerberg into the public school system in Newark, New Jersey, a city with a population of just 275,000 people, has had only negligible impact in improving the outcomes of that suffering school district.[3] Our political system is awash in unregulated cash, and our politicians have lost the ability to compromise, let alone even agree what the problems are that they aren't solving. Everywhere we look we see landscapes of real need littered with the wreckage of dysfunctional or broken systems: our public infrastructure, health care, food systems, extremist terrorism, criminal justice, waste disposal...the list goes on and on. "This century is broken," *New York Times* columnist David Brooks audaciously declared in a 2017 headline to an opinion piece written less than twenty years into the new century.

An internet search for the phrase *broken systems* links to articles on global warming, economic inequality, health care, the legislative process, public education, criminal justice, and even college sports. It seems as though the more information we possess, the less effective we are. This queasy, overwhelmed feeling that keeps us up at night wondering what to do is a symptom of our maladaptation to a context where the rules are bending in unexpected ways and we are, like roller skaters on an ice rink, struggling to make any forward progress. In many ways it is a result of the wild interconnectedness of the wired world: When most everything is tangled with something else in some way or another, it is nearly impossible to stop untying knots, and even harder to know where to begin.

So, why is scale a component in all these diverse dilemmas? The short answer is that the world has become unruly... or has become unruly in new ways. This is, in part, the result of two important shifts, what I will call immateriality and entanglement. The first, immateriality, results from the digital processes by which we have turned atoms into bits—as Nicholas Negroponte phrased it—or compasses into apps. It has turned things that were hard, physical, and graspable into invisible, immaterial flows of ones and zeroes, ons and offs. *Documents, files,* and *photos* are now invisible pulses of electricity captured on magnetic media and visualized by infinitesimal pixels on a screen instead of yellowed, dog-eared artifacts that we shove in a desk drawer or shoebox.

And this dematerialization is not just affecting physical matter. Services, as well, are increasingly immaterial. Banks, for instance, are rethinking their entire service offerings in light of this shift. As recently as forty years ago banks were still erecting monumental, granite edifices to symbolize their solidity, their grandeur, and their permanence. Today, most of those buildings house restaurants. Meanwhile, the banks themselves (now multinational conglomerates) are struggling to figure out how to connect to Generation Z, the emerging demographic group that expects banking to be at their thumbtips, a mere matter of zapping electrons from one account to another. This is a paradigmatic shift in our sensory world, the impact and effects of which we are only starting to understand.

The second factor, entanglement, is the rise of interconnected and essential networks that have become the infrastructure of our everyday lives. Because our systems are so interlinked, the individual has become—paradoxically—both uniquely empowered and hopelessly overmatched. Consider a young couple looking to secure a mortgage in a midsized town in Massachusetts. Thirty years ago, that couple would have gone to a local bank, met with a loan officer whose family they might already know, and discussed the range of interest rates that the bank could offer for a property situated within a stable community. Most, if not all, of that transaction would have been determined by the dynamics of the local context, for better or worse (and certainly redlining and other forms of face-to-face, legalized discrimination made it worse for minority populations). Transpose this scene to 2008, though, and a vastly different picture emerges. First of all, the couple might simply have applied for the mortgage online and never actually met the broker (who might be situated in a call center continents away). Their mortgage offer would likely be bundled together with hundreds of other mortgages into a complex financial instrument called a mortgage-backed security. That mortgage-backed security would then be sold to a global market of investors who were looking to skim additional value off of it. The stability of the mortgage could end up being influenced by economic decisions in Greece, China, and almost everywhere else on the globe. Once that system melted down in 2008, and the value of people's properties were worth less than their outstanding debt, it didn't much matter if your daughter played on your banker's daughter's soccer team, because neither of you had much influence on the valuation or the situation. After 2008, many homeowners were underwater (as they say in the home loan business), drowning in the complexity of the networked world, inexplicably overwhelmed by the decisions of actors from countries thousands of miles away.

Or consider the computer hacker, able to cripple a major international bank by himself. The idea that one lone individual could intentionally hack into a corporate giant like a bank or financial services company was utterly unimaginable only a generation ago, or at least lived only in Hollywood fantasies. Now it has become commonplace. Individuals and small groups of cybercriminals are breaking into global, transnational corporations like Sony and "impenetrable" national organizations like the Pentagon with apparent ease, mucking about in their servers, destabilizing their information architecture, or pilfering their "secure" data and selling it on the dark web—the digital equivalent of the black market. The networked, digital communications infrastructure laid upon the creaky, physical infrastructure of the nineteenth and twentieth centuries has produced a monstrous hybrid that has us entangled in its maw. We feel alternately all-powerful and overwhelmed in the face of this crossbred condition. At the precise moment when a vast and dazzling world is at our fingertips, our noses are pressed to the glass of our computer screens and our fingertips are able to know it only through keystrokes and made-up hand gestures (pinch and zoom, double tap, four-finger swipe).

If the first dizzying shift is the result of the digital dematerialization of our artifacts, processes, and services, then the second shift reflects the vast infrastructure of interconnectedness that we've built. We once built farms, highways, and pipelines. Today, we are building server farms, information superhighways, and data pipelines. It's as if we're seeding, cultivating, and harvesting information relays (and perhaps we are already) instead of living systems. We're trapped in limbo, adrift in the layers between the physical and the digital. This condition of feeling caught between two worlds—each with its own rules and logics—is cleverly captured by the artist Aram Bartholl in his project *Map*.

Fig. 3. *Aram Bartholl,* Map, *2006–19, sculpture, steel, aluminum mesh, steel cables 900 x 520 x 20 cm, Taipei, 2010.*

In this project, Bartholl reverses the direction of most changes that we encounter: He makes the digital physical. He installs twenty-foot-tall Google Maps pointers—the twenty-pixel, red, teardrop-shaped locator flags in digital map services—in actual locations in cities, towns, and public spaces. Bartholl's installations remind us that we now move through space that is simultaneously physical and digital, and that we are having a harder time keeping the two straight.

Virtual, augmented, and mixed realities will only intensify this interleaving. We seem to exist now at the diaphanous membrane between the physical and the digital—between the world and its digital double. By layering a real interpretation of the digital upon our real, so to speak, Bartholl inverts our expectations and throws our conceptual boundaries askew, revealing the very strangeness of this hybrid world we're building.

Ironically, what makes our uneasy relationship to scale so unsettling and resonant is that we do think in scales all the time, whether we are aware of it or not: Measuring ingredients to mix a cocktail, deciding whether to lift up a small child, observing the speed limit while driving on the highway, and picking out a pair of shoes that fit properly are all exercises in scalar judgment. But scale can also be a means for thinking through the relationship of the small to the large, or the representation (or model) to the represented. In architecture, for instance, scale models are tools for architects to assemble, examine, analyze, and even experience space and materials. The cost of building at full scale is prohibitive, so an architect builds a smaller, proportionally accurate version of it as a proxy for the full experience. Business models, as well, are less data-rich schemas for what a business is or will be shaped like. Scale models, in this sense, are mimetic: They mirror the real thing, though they are reduced in sensory data.

To think in scales, then, is to adopt a process of reasoning that extrapolates from the small to the large, from the reduced to the full, and from the incomplete to the complete. We project into the model the attributes of the fully realized thing itself, and vice versa. When anthropologists and sociologists deduce culture-wide patterns of behavior and meaning from the actions of a few individuals, are they not also thinking in scales—deriving properties of the whole culture from an analysis of a part? Scale, in this sense, suffuses our thought processes, though we might not think of it that way.

To understand the puzzling forces that are deforming our everyday experiences, we will need to venture deep into the very idea of scale. To understand it better, and to learn how to navigate it more effectively, this book takes form in two parts. The first part is more anecdotal and analytical. The first four chapters will, themselves, shift across increasing scales so that we may better understand not only how scale works but also how it is changing. We start with measurement and the hazards of quantitative thinking. From there we consider the human figure and its modern struggle to thrive in the new environments that technology creates. We explore how we learn scale and what it feels like. From the figure we'll move to the system. It's impossible to understand our own quixotic relation to the scale of things today without thinking in systems, as the systems guru Donella Meadows would suggest, and recognizing the ways in which changes in scale can precipitate unexpected system behaviors. And finally, we discover how networks have created the conditions for upending our very understanding of cause and effect. Small actions and actors can seem to have monumental impact, and our collective will to improve the systems around us often gets us nowhere.

The first half of the book helps us to understand the surprising behaviors that live within scale, and the second half outlines tactics and strategies for navigating more effectively this impossible present. In other words, we have to first understand our context before we can remedy it. Are there approaches, or even "acupuncture points," that will yield results once we understand better the complexities of scale? In the second half I introduce four strategies: giving form to the formless, scalar framing, scaffolding, and embracing complexity. Together, these are means by which we can take positive steps forward that acknowledge our unsettled condition while thinking *through* scale, not fighting against it. These insights will work in business, management, policy, design, social innovation, and any other fields that are confronting complex, systemic change and feeling pressure to make things happen in new ways. There are no easy answers for resolving the "wicked problems" that haunt our age, but there are frameworks we can lean on when little else seems to work—schemas for action in the face of uncertainty.

Scale reveals its effects in unexpected places and in ephemeral ways. Simply being able to *see* scale and its deforming effects is the primary goal of this book. To see it more clearly, I have brought together unlike things and put them into the same frame, revealing unlikely parallels, unanticipated resonances, and unexpected opportunities. It is precisely this condition that French philosopher Michel Foucault wrangled with in the Introduction to his archaeology of the human sciences titled *The Order of Things*. To illustrate this, Foucault drew upon a fragment of fiction written by the Argentine writer Jorge Luis Borges. In his writing, Borges bends rationality and science to its breaking point: Uncanny ideas and disorienting dilemmas seep out through the cracks and fissures he creates. Erudite and mischievous, Borges's fiction hovers in the uncanny valley between knowledge and its undoing. Foucault, in this work, is attempting to illustrate that categories of Western thought are, themselves, artificial—they are symptoms of how power becomes knowledge. Striving to find a way in his opening paragraphs to communicate the strange and deceptive permanence of these categories, Foucault infamously invokes a now-legendary passage from Borges to argue for the illusoriness of those permanent-seeming categories,

This book first arose out of a passage in [Jorge Luis] Borges, out of the laughter that shattered, as I read the passage, all the familiar landmarks of my thought—*our* thought that bears the stamp of our age and our geography—breaking up all the ordered surfaces and all the planes with which we are accustomed to tame the wild profusion of existing things, and continuing long afterwards to disturb and threaten with collapse our age-old distinction between the Same and the Other. This passage quotes a "certain Chinese

encyclopaedia" in which it is written that "animals
are divided into: (a) belonging to the Emperor, (b)
embalmed, (c) tame, (d) suckling pigs, (e) sirens, (f)
fabulous, (g) stray dogs, (h) included in the present
classification, (i) frenzied, (j) innumerable, (k) drawn
with a very fine camelhair brush, (l) *et cetera*, (m) having just broken the water pitcher, (n) that from a long
way off look like flies." In the wonderment of this
taxonomy, the thing we apprehend in one great leap,
the thing that, by means of the fable, is demonstrated
as the exotic charm of another system of thought, is
the limitation of our own, the stark impossibility of
thinking *that*.[4]

Not to Scale puts together into the same frame bubble
levels and garden gnomes; quantum mechanics and traffic
circles; the Linux operating system and IKEA catalogs; feral
pigs and NATO's Afghanistan plan; big data and tiny ants.
Scale is unruly. Our lives are unruly. Scale contributes to that.
Along the way, if nothing else, I hope that the reader will, at
times, encounter the limitation of her own thought...as well
as the stark possibility of thinking *that*.

Chapter 01

On Exactitude in Science

Nigel Tufnel is an engagingly daft guitarist in a British heavy metal band. Marty DeBergi, a documentary filmmaker, is following him and his bandmates, capturing with his film crew the exploits of this declining, hapless rock band, called Spinal Tap. In one scene, after proudly showing off several of his prize guitars to Marty, Nigel drags him over to examine a very special Marshall amplifier:

> **Nigel:** This is a top to a, you know, what we use on stage, but it's very...very special because if you can see—
> **Marty:** Yeah.
> **Nigel:** —the numbers all go to 11.[...]Look...right across the board.
> **Marty:** Ahh...oh, I see—
> **Nigel:** 11...11...11...
> **Marty:** —and most of these amps go up to 10...

Nigel: Exactly.

Marty: Does that mean it's...louder? Is it any louder?

Nigel: Well, it's one louder, isn't it? It's not 10. You see, most...most blokes, you know, will be playing at 10. You're on 10 here...all the way up...all the way up—

Marty: Yeah.

Nigel: —all the way up. You're on 10 on your guitar... where can you go from there? Where?

Marty: I don't know.

Nigel: Nowhere. Exactly. What we do is if we need that extra...push over the cliff...you know what we do?

Marty: Put it up to 11.

Nigel: 11. Exactly. One louder.

Marty: Why don't you just make 10 louder and make 10 be the top...number...and make that a little louder?

[*pause*]

Nigel: These go to 11.[1]

This ridiculously funny and now legendary exchange from the fake documentary film *This Is Spinal Tap* gleefully skewers the vanity and pomposity of the heavy metal rock scene, while also serving as a parody of self-serious documentaries. But remarkably, this goofy exchange also reveals a world. Unexpectedly, through the course of this dialogue, we are privy to a discussion about the very nature of scale and how it shapes our perceptions of the sounds, objects, and environments around us.

Fig. 4. *Film still,* This Is Spinal Tap. *Courtesy of STUDIOCANAL.*

In this debate, the character of Nigel Tufnel takes the point of view of what philosophers might call a metaphysical naturalist. He argues, in effect, that the numerical scale on the amplifier's knobs points to a real, fixed framework: 10 will always sound as loud as 10...and 11 will always be one louder. Marty DeBergi, in contrast, challenges the very essence of the numbers themselves. He questions whether the amplifier's markings ultimately refer to anything in particular in the world beyond themselves, and whether the numbers are, instead, a construct of human origin. DeBergi, in the end, appears to have the upper hand in this disagreement. Scale is very much a human construct, but one that is built upon a foundation of measurement.

What are 10 and 11 really pointing to, anyway? Decibels? Certainly not. Whether we are choosing between wearing a parka or a sweater, purchasing a package of coffee beans, trying to obey the speed limit, or turning up the volume one more notch, we glide along various scales constantly throughout our day. In these guises, scale is hardly mysterious or even interesting. It is simply a nonphysical, quantitative infrastructure that is built upon measurement and that helps to give form to otherwise formless experiences: We may not be able to feel the difference between driving forty-eight and sixty-five miles per hour, but the speedometer and the posted speed limits allow civil society to regulate drivers' recklessness in the interest of greater safety to all... provided that your fifty-five miles per hour is the same as mine.

All of this would seem to suggest that there is nothing particularly interesting or even noteworthy about scale as a concept. We cohabitate with it quite happily, and it presents few evident problems to us. We assume that measurement is inviolable and exact, the outcome of scientific processes that are themselves foolproof. The search for precise and accurate measurement has a complex and tortuous history. Scratch the surface and there are surprises and eccentricities that reveal a wobbly ground upon which to build a foundation of scalar thinking.

Measurement is, in some ways, the guarantor of quantitative scale. Without quantitative measure, we find ourselves in the fuzzier world of qualitative, subjective comparison: Is this beer more pleasantly bitter than that one? Is that chili pepper hotter than this one? Remarkably, in the absence of quantitative scales, we often invent them. Beer brewers have developed a standard called IBUs (international bitterness units) in order to reliably compare the bitterness of beer. Hot pepper aficionados have come up with SHUs (Scoville Heat units) to quantify the difference between the prickly heat of a jalapeno and the scorching heat of a Carolina reaper. In each case, the reliability of units of measure depends upon reproducible science: IBUs represent the presence in parts per million of isohumulone, an acid found in hops;[2] and scientists now determine the value of SHUs through a process known as high-performance liquid chromatography (HPLC), which tests for the presence of the chemical capsaicin, the source of heat in peppers. HPLC replaced the original test of SHUs, called the Scoville Organoleptic Test, which consisted of diluting equal amounts of peppers with sugar water until the testers could no longer discern any heat.[3] But our perception of bitterness in beers is, in fact, highly dependent upon the other ingredients: The more malt in a beer, the less we taste "bitter," regardless of IBUs. And two identical-looking habanero peppers might have significantly different SHUs, dependent upon where, when, and how they are grown. Try as we might to measure the known world—to really know it—the act of measurement often seems to come up just short.

———

In February of 2011, Sarah Lyall of the *New York Times* reported that the world standard for the kilogram had, in fact, lost weight. "The change, discovered when the prototype was compared with its official copies, amounts only to some 50 micrograms, equal to the mass of a smallish grain of sand. But it shows that the prototype has fallen down on its primary job, to be a beacon of stability in a world of uncertainty."[4] In order to fully fathom the radical implications of this discovery, it is essential to restate that this one, singular, alloyed piece of cast platinum-iridium is *the* kilogram—that is, there is no other standard existing in the world that can serve as the guarantor of everything that we weigh. It is one of the oddest tautologies of our modern existence: The mass of a kilogram is equal to the mass of *that* kilogram, locked under three glass bell jars in a basement in Sèvres, France … and accessible only when each of the three key holders to the safe room are present to unlock the door. Unlike the meter and liter, which the international community of metrologists replaced with other, less unstable standards, this primordial chunk of metal is the ultimate means by which we know what a kilogram actually is. And that singular, polished cylinder of metal, whose height is roughly equal to its width, has been doing its job since 1889, when the International Bureau of Weights and Measures (BIPM) came together (after decades of politicking and disagreement) to designate it as the standard. The immediate question that must arise is, "How did they know that it weighed a kilogram?" Against what was it measured? The philosopher Ludwig Wittgenstein playfully described that same dilemma with respect to the standard meter when he suggested, in his book *Philosophical Investigations*, "There is one thing of which one can say neither that it is one meter long, nor that it is not one meter long, and that is the standard meter in Paris." And as Lyall's reporting points out, scientists verify the mass of the kilogram, remarkably, by measuring it against copies of itself, which pushes the tautology even further. And consider the implications of this discovery: If the universal standard for mass is no longer itself, what does that mean for all its official copies? Are they still copies? And what, in fact, do they weigh? A kilogram? Fifty micrograms more than a kilogram?

This peculiar problem has bedeviled scientists for decades. The search for precision and universality in weights and measures—the scales by which we comprehend quantity in our world—is a surprisingly young science, and the universal standards around which we base our scientific discoveries and our international trade are younger still. One imagines that these scales would have been set in stone, literally, for centuries, but that is hardly the case. The very first national law of any kind in the United States to establish a system of measure as "official" was enacted in 1866, stating that "from and after the passage of this Act it shall be lawful throughout the United States of America to employ the weights and measures of the metric system."[5] That is not a misprint: The very first law that Congress passed standardizing weights and measures utilized the metric system as its standard, even though the United States was using the imperial system of measure across the country. The metric system, at that time, was a more fully standardized system, so the U.S. government used it as a benchmark even though it was not the measuring system of the land.

The development of standards was not simply a matter for science and trade. As John Quincy Adams pointed out decades before that in a report to Congress of 1821, there is a moral component to the quest for regular, repeatable, and uniform scales:

> Weights and measures may be ranked among the necessaries of life to every individual of human society. They enter into the economical arrangements and daily concerns of every family. They are necessary to every occupation of human industry; to the distribution and security of every species of property; to every transaction of trade and commerce; to the labors of the husbandman; to the ingenuity of the artificer; to the studies of the philosopher; to the researches of the antiquarian; to the navigation of the mariner; and the marches of the soldier; to all the exchanges of peace, and all the operations of war. The knowledge of them, as in established use, is among the first elements of education, and is often learned by those who learn nothing else, not even to read and write. The knowledge is riveted in the memory by the habitual application of it to the employments of men throughout life.[6]

Despite his passionate argument, well into the twentieth century scientists were still at odds over what constituted a basic and verifiable unit of measure. Most of the major international accords that put into place universal standards were not reached until much later than Adams's time, and the search for less unstable constants continues today.

The General Conference on Weights and Measures (CGPM), the international body that establishes the scales we live by, created in 1960 the International System of Units (SI). The CGPM then established the International Bureau of Weights and Measures, whose work it is to define and verify the system of units. Its findings are the basis upon which we measure ourselves and the world around us. The BIPM has thus far instituted seven basic, standard units: the meter (length), the kilogram (mass), the second (time), the ampere (electric current), the kelvin (thermodynamic temperature), the mole (amount of substance), and the candela (the unit of luminous intensity). The SI defines the candela as "the luminous intensity, in a given direction, of a source that emits monochromatic radiation of frequency 540×10^{12} hertz and that has a radiant intensity in that direction of $1/683$ watt per steradian." It defines the ampere as "that constant current which, if maintained in two straight parallel conductors of infinite length, of negligible circular cross-section, and placed 1 metre apart in vacuum, would produce between these conductors a force equal to 2×10^{-7} newton per metre of length."

And, despite decades of searching by scientists to find a physical standard, it defines the kilogram as follows: "The kilogram is the unit of mass; it is equal to the mass of the international prototype of the kilogram."[7] One of these things is, evidently, not like the others. The kilogram is the only remaining SI unit of measure that is based upon a physical, existing reference prototype. It is a thing itself. It is what it is. For all other standards, scientists have determined "physical" standards of measure that they base not on tautologies but, instead, upon processes that scientists anywhere in the world can reliably repeat (without needing recourse to a physical artifact).[8]

Robert Crease, in his fascinating history of the search for measurement absolutes, *The World in the Balance*, details the scientific community's efforts to define, with precision and certitude, the standards that comprise our systems of measurement. These struggles have taken two forms: the technical quest to establish universal and absolute means to define the units themselves; and the political struggles within the international community to adopt systems that all countries around the globe could utilize consistently. We have had provincial systems to weigh pigs and measure out ale and determine miles traveled for thousands of years, but these have typically differed from country to country, town to town, and even feudal lord to feudal lord. Those of us growing up under the imperial system of measure all know, at least anecdotally, something of the origin of the units of measure themselves. We've grown up with stories of units of measure that capriciously derived from the limbs of rulers (and now the double meaning of the word *ruler* becomes more vivid), and how the "foot" varied from one sovereign to the next, depending on little more than the relative size of his feet. From a mouthful to a handful or from a nail to a hand, imperial and Roman scales nearly all trace their origins back to the human body in one way or another. This is true for Chinese measurement systems as well, as the human body set the standards for the *chi* (a foot measure) and the *cun* (a finger measure), which date from at least 400 BCE.[9] Many people throughout history have understood the urgent need to develop systems of measure that are inviolable and constant, but it took the persistence and determination of the French in the eighteenth century to push us toward the metric system that forms the basis of the SI system that fifty-nine member states and forty-two associate states have adopted as recently as 2018.[10]

Initially, the development of the metric system replaced body-based measurements with standards built upon seemingly immutable, *physical* constants. A standard of length—the meter—anchors the process, as it is possible to then derive mass (kilogram: the weight of a cubic decimeter of water) and volume (liter: a cubic decimeter) from it. French scientists' early attempts to fix the meter to a fraction of Earth's meridian led to the creation of the first universalizing, fixed standards: a meter-long platinum bar and a kilogram-heavy platinum cylinder. Each was the first step in creating a system that one could tie directly to physical constants (in the case of the meter, it was derived from 1/5,130,740 of a meridian quadrant).[11] This was a paradigmatic leap in the history of measurement. While it still did not have international agreement (that was to come much later), the accomplishment of creating a reference standard that was no longer tied to the human body but instead to something constant everywhere created a precise frame of reference that could, theoretically, be replicated by anybody, anywhere, at any time.

Ironically, however, it was not so much the process that became the standard, as was the intent, but the heavily secured platinum artifacts. The predicament, of course, was that despite its seeming permanence, even a pristinely polished platinum artifact will eventually suffer from physical breakdown and nearly immeasurable accumulation. Whether through the introduction of impurities in the casting process, the creation of air bubbles within the alloy, or the accumulation of daily grit and grime, physical artifacts are prone to the vicissitudes of our modern, messy existence. The SI definition of the kilogram, for instance, also includes this surprising housekeeping instruction: "However, due to the inevitable accumulation of contaminants on surfaces, the international prototype is subject to reversible surface contamination that approaches 1 μg per year in mass. For this reason, the CIPM declared that, pending further research, the reference mass of the international prototype is that immediately after cleaning and washing by a specified method."[12] Thus, our lonely kilogram has a regular bath, removing the trace contaminants that muck up its whole rationale.

It is for this reason that metrologists have sought, and have now confirmed for the other six units, "physical constants" to define the basic units of measurement. This search began with the meter, not coincidentally, which the BIPM has defined since 1960 in relation not to the bars of alloyed metals but instead to a "length equal to 1650763.73 wavelengths in vacuum of the radiation corresponding to the transition between the levels $2p_{10}$ and $5d_5$, of the krypton-86 atom." Or as they updated it in 1983, "the length of the path traveled by light in vacuum during a time interval of 1/299,792,458 of a second."[13] Whereas, at one point in time, the yard was roughly equivalent to the distance between the nose and one's outstretched fingertip, this turn toward physical constants recalibrated this distance in ways that only instruments can know. The human brain cannot perceive intervals that approach 1/300,000,000 of a second, and we do not live in a vacuum. Under this system, we can use only intermediating instruments to verify what we want to know to be true. In this way, scientific progress in measurement has been a long march to decenter the human body and human perception from our systems of measure. No longer are we—like Leonardo's Vitruvian Man—at the center of the knowledge ordering system.

The argument that John Quincy Adams passionately makes—that uniform and verifiable systems of scale are at the heart of a civil, functioning, and just society—ripples through the lament that the journalist Sarah Lyall makes about the kilogram's loss of mass: "The prototype has fallen down on its primary job, to be a beacon of stability in a world of uncertainty." In an uncertain world, we grasp at those things that provide constancy, steadiness, and assuredness. The quest for accurate and universal systems of measure may seem like an enterprise of interest only to scientists and bureaucrats, but there is something deeper at play that Adams's quote brings to the surface. Fairness, justice, and equality are also, to some extent, measures of things. Blind Justice, of course, holds a scale in her hand. There is a moral quality to measurement that floats just above arguments about precision and accuracy. The distancing of measurement from the human body and human experience will undoubtedly yield greater precision, but what happens as we lose touch, literally, with the frameworks that shape our world?

———

Kern is a seventh generation, family-operated German company that specializes in the manufacture and sale of precision scales. Started in 1844, Kern has built its reputation on a combination of precision German engineering and solid reliability. So, it was perhaps a bit of a surprise when Kern embarked on a whimsical experiment to explore variations in gravity on Earth's surface using a Kern model EWB 2.4 scale carefully packed into a protective suitcase nestled right next to an equally padded little garden gnome named, self-referentially, Kern.

Fig. 5. *Gnome Kit from Kern's "The Gnome Experiment."*

Most of us assume that we weigh the same amount whether we take that measurement in Lima, Peru, Addis Ababa, Ethiopia, or Singapore, but that is actually not the case. For gravity to be constant everywhere on Earth's surface, Earth would need to be a perfect sphere of uniform density, and it is not. Instead, it takes the shape of an oblate spheroid, slightly flatter at the poles while bulging out a bit at the equator. It is more "potato shaped," claims Kern's general manager, Albert Sauter, in their uncharacteristically spirited promotional video for the Gnome Experiment.[14] In order to understand more precisely the variations in gravity and its effect on our weight, Kern—in a promotional campaign devised by the advertising agency Ogilvy & Mather—invited scientists from around the world to weigh Kern, the garden gnome (made from "a special chip-proof resin"), who hails from the same southwestern part of Germany that Kern does, and to pin its weight on a global map. Garden gnomes, Kern suggests, do not gain and lose weight, so they are excellent constants for weighing (and they make a bigger PR bang than a platinum-iridium cylinder).

The results that have come in show significant variation. At the South Pole, Kern weighed in at 309.82 grams, its heaviest anywhere, as expected. At the equator in Nanyuki, Kenya, Kern balanced out at a slim 307.52 grams, almost three-quarters of 1 percent lighter. The bulge at the equator puts Kern at its greatest distance from the center of Earth, and Nanyuki is itself at 6,388 feet of elevation, which explains why the gnome is so lightweight. What the Gnome Experiment cleverly reveals is that we take for granted the idea that the forces that determine our physical properties and, therefore, our scales, are consistent and uniform around the globe...that a kilogram in London is a kilogram in Nanyuki. The remarkably significant variation that the Kern Gnome Experiment reveals tells us that a force such as gravity varies considerably with geography, because the distance to Earth's center varies, because Earth is not a perfect sphere of uniform density, and in slight ways because the moon and sun exert their own gravitational influences. Consider the implication for *the* kilogram, then. It does not follow that what weighs one kilogram in Sèvres, France, would weigh the same thing even just one country away. For example, Kern the Gnome weighed

308.26 grams in Balingen, Germany (his home), but weighed just 307.65 grams in Geneva, Switzerland, at the headquarters of the Large Hadron Collider at CERN.

This point—that science can seem less exact the closer we look—is probably more of a surprise to nonscientists than it is to the scientific community itself. Nonspecialists typically assume that scientific practices are exact, absolute, and unwavering. In fact, they are surprisingly fuzzy and full of uncertainty. As we have seen, even something as foundational as measurement is rife with peculiarities and irregularities, so that much of which we take for granted based on our own human experience is almost false, mostly false, or a little false. Scientists, in many instances, can actually quantify their degree of uncertainty, which certainly separates them from most of us. But even so, that doesn't mean that they don't also have to learn to thrive in conditions where doubt and the unknown are part of the ground they stand on.

———

How unreliable is measurement? Why is it that with each closer look it seems to become less dependable? With an accurate measuring instrument, surely, it would be possible to measure things accurately, or so the metrological evangelists must have believed. But things are rarely so straightforward. Lewis Fry Richardson is a remarkable figure in the history of mathematics, and the source of one of the most vexing paradoxes of measurement. A man of Quaker beliefs, he was a pacifist and a conscientious objector, refusing to serve in World War I, though he did enroll with a Quaker Friends Ambulance Unit working with the Sixteenth French Infantry.[15] His moral compass was strong, and he even refused to practice his own mathematical trade during the conflict lest his efforts inadvertently support the Commonwealth's war effort. Richardson's real gift, though, was applying mathematical concepts and differential equations to phenomena that appeared, at first glance, to defy mathematical description. In other words, he quantified the qualitative.

As a pacifist, Richardson also sought ways to understand war and violence through the lens that made the most sense to him—mathematics. He published articles in which he identified significant, quantifiable factors—misunderstandings, warlike attitudes, size of armies, and even lengths of adjoining borders—that, when correlated together into mathematical models, could predict the likelihood of war between two nations. It was while researching border lengths between countries that he stumbled upon a puzzling anomaly: Very often, two different countries had dramatically different measurements of their shared border.

It turns out that the tools used to measure irregular boundaries like borders and coastlines can actually alter the length itself. Fry's discovery led to what we now call the coastline paradox. Simply put, the paradox is that the longer one's measuring unit, the shorter the distance measured. Imagine, for a moment, that one is trying to measure the craggy coastline of Maine. Using a map and a one-mile long unit, the coastline would appear to be 3,478 miles (according to World Atlas.com). But if one were measuring it with a one-foot-long ruler—and able to trace all the cragginess of even individual rocks in very fine detail—the coast would *be* much longer. A longer measuring "stick" cannot navigate the smaller twists and turns that a shorter measuring stick can. A measuring unit smaller than a grain of sand would account for every out-cropping on every grain of sand, making the coast even longer. And a quantum measuring stick could measure the space between atoms...and so forth. Like a fractal, each successive zoom in to a closer scale reveals the same relationship over and over again. The length of the measuring unit is inversely proportional to the total length of the coastline, it turns out. What this means, in a deeper, philosophical sense, is that the length of the coastline is, in some sense, unknowable. This does not mean that we cannot measure length. But it does mean that how we measure has everything to do with the outcomes we produce.[16]

Our measurement of time, too, is not immune to variability. And, yet again, the BIPM plays a pivotal role in how we understand time and its wrinkles. The BIPM identifies and defines the second as the basis upon which we measure duration. That definition—"the duration of 9,192,631,770 periods of the radiation corresponding to the transition between the two hyperfine levels of the ground state of the caesium 133 atom"—does not relate either to human perception or, more significant, in any direct way to the rotation of Earth, the ground that once seemed to anchor our Western notions of time. In 1970 the BIPM decoupled our measure of time from Earth's rotation because that rotation was actually slowing down and, as a result, became scientifically unreliable. It is important to note that the creation of a standard unit, the second, and a means to determine its duration does not give us an actual account of what time it is. For that, the BIPM has created International Atomic Time (TAI), which is its best calculation of the time on Earth right now.[17]

To create TAI, the BIPM determines a weighted average of readings taken by more than four hundred atomic clocks at over eighty laboratories across the world. The average is weighted in part because the laboratories' heights above sea level can affect their readings (just as we saw with Kern's Gnome Experiment). But TAI also does not quite align with Earth's rotation. Thus, we have the existence of Coordinated Universal Time (UTC), which is effectively a combination of TAI and Greenwich Mean Time (GMT): "To compensate for Earth's irregular velocity of rotation, the International Telecommunication Union (ITU) defined in 1972 a procedure for adding (or suppressing) a second as necessary, to ensure that the difference between the international time reference and rotational time remained less than 0.9 s[econd]. The resulting time scale is Coordinated Universal Time (UTC)." This 0.9 second is the infamous "leap second," which the BIPM added on the last day of 2016. The existence of a leap second has led to a chronic misalignment between UTC and TAI: "The difference between Coordinated Universal Time (UTC) and International Atomic Time (TAI) will then be –37 s[econds] until further notice."[18] It is worth noting that there is also Universal Time (based on astronomical phenomena), Standard Time (the reference time that most of us use, and based upon geography and the sun's movement), Terrestrial Time (used by astronomers to measure the movement of other bodies in space), and System Time (a chronological framework that computers utilize, usually set to count a series of "ticks" from the first moment an operating system goes live).[19]

All of this hardly suggests that time, as it plays its role in modern society, is an illusion. But as with spatial measurement systems, the science is not nearly as reassuring as we might imagine. Measurement, and our urge to create quantities out of qualities, is likely never going to be a perfect science. Measurement is in many ways predicated upon an assumption that we can separate a thing from its surroundings, define its boundaries clearly, isolate it, and, finally, submit it to the will of our quantifying instruments, as if we will encounter no hazards in that process. Systems thinking would suggest that we cannot know a *thing* without also knowing all that it is tangled up and enmeshed with. When we isolate it in order to measure, we separate it from its context. Perhaps this is why our systems of measure are so fuzzy. Their imprecision reminds us that the world and our experiences will not submit peacefully to being counted up, and that there is a rending form of turbulence that occurs when we isolate things from contexts, or figures from grounds (as we explore later). The shift from qualities to quantities is, in some ways, the story of civilization. Mathematics, monetary systems, and double-entry bookkeeping were all pivotal innovations that fundamentally changed the possible. But the journey toward finer and finer precision in measurement also reflects a drift of knowledge away from our bodies, away from our senses, and just a little further away from the messiness of who we are.

Chapter 02

The Figure and the Ground

It is an extraordinary experience to hear a church organ rumble in an age-old cathedral. The sound that emanates from it when it hits its deepest, most resonant tones is staggering—literally. The air seems to pulsate and the notes to reverberate from within the body. It is a physical, awe-inspiring experience. One can only imagine how a churchgoer in the early modern years—before electricity and amplification—would have experienced those same notes. It must have been utterly commanding, perhaps only comparable to the sound of thunder. Hearing it today, it is still hard not to be transported by it, to lose oneself in the awesome power and majesty of it. It's clear just what a powerful recruitment tool the church organ must have been: Its deep, sonorous volume could overtake the body and, perhaps, move the soul.

When we are overcome by forces that flood our senses, we are reminded of our own fragility and, perhaps, even our mortality. Our tendency is to pull inward, shut down, or even flee. Religions and the state have used scale and spectacle throughout history to subjugate citizens or awe them with majesty—think palaces, military parades, and cathedrals. It is through a sense of scale that we make sense of the world. There are physical and even psychological effects to scale, and there is a history to our encounters with it. It's no coincidence that theories of alienation and shell shock emerged at the same time as the rise of the industrial age when massive machines, mechanized warfare, and demoralizing factory work assaulted the individual. And we will encounter again the impact of scale changes when we try to understand why we are feeling so unmoored in our own, immaterially entangled present. Our environment is changing once again, and with it comes a whole new set of perceptual and conceptual challenges. To understand them, we will try to track the complex and intimate relationship between the individual and the scale of her surroundings in order to understand more effectively the role of scale in shaping who we are.

Artists, social critics, and philosophers of the late nineteenth and early twentieth centuries connected the overwhelming mechanization and electrification of our cities to the alienation of the individual. The huge migrations of rural natives to cities during the industrial revolution created an influx of people who were likely unprepared for the massive buildings, clamoring construction equipment, hissing factory floors, and prodigious pollution belched out by factories. Not coincidentally, it was at this same time that Sigmund Freud posited our alienation from our own egos in the form of the unconscious and Karl Marx diagnosed capitalism's capacity to alienate us from our labor. But it was particularly the scale of colossal urban infrastructure, electrified nighttime, a hyperkinetic pace, and mechanical forms of transportation that created sensory environments that shocked and unsettled human experience. In 1939 the German social philosopher Walter Benjamin wandered the bustling boulevards of European cities in search of a philosophy that could redeem the human subject disordered by the mechanized chaos. He wrote, "Moving through this traffic involves the individual in a series of shocks and collisions. At dangerous intersections, nervous impulses flow through him in rapid succession, like the energy from a battery. Baudelaire speaks of a man who plunges into the crowd as into a reservoir of electric energy. Circumscribing the experience of the shock, he calls this man 'a *kaleidoscope* equipped with consciousness.'"[1]

Freud, Marx, and Benjamin captured with their writing a condition where the environmental surround was consuming the individual, leaving a shattered, "kaleidoscopic" consciousness in its wake—ecstasy, hallucination, reverie, dream, dissociation, psychosis. The new arrivals to these rapidly transforming cities were losing themselves in the chaos, overcome by the heights of the buildings, the volume of the noise, and the intensity of the experiences—these "nervous impulses." The dissociation of the self into its surroundings—the loosening of the ego—took on forms ranging from alienation to shell shock to madness and other neurasthenic symptoms. These feelings of loss, disorientation, and confusion—but also excitement and stimulation—led to movements such as the Futurists and the Surrealists, whose members used these new sentiments and sensory stimuli as starting points for their work.

One can also trace the origin of the management sciences to this same era, and to the same sense of not quite fitting in. Industrial engineers such as Frederick W. Taylor were trying to reconcile our human capabilities to those of the machines that were increasingly shaping the work environment. In the film *Modern Times*, Charlie Chaplin made a mockery of our assimilation to the machines, as he himself (representing the typical assembly line worker) gets caught up like a cog in the gears of the machine. But researchers such as Taylor were striving to find the optimal fit between the opportunities of these new, miraculous machines and the capabilities of the humans who labored beside them. Taylor broke tasks down into their component parts, measured the duration of time it took to effectively complete them, and developed rules and protocols that maximized efficiency, often at the expense of the workers' own well-being. In other words, he tried to fit the human worker to the pace, the power, and the scale of the factory machines.

———

Scale follows us like a shadow. It is tied to our bodies, and yet it has no real substance. We make it, or cast it, as a spectral by-product of who we are. Scale lacks substance. It is a construct of our own creation. Yet it, too, seems to follow us wherever we go. Our capacity to orient and ground ourselves against the surround is one of the anchors that keeps us in the here and now; it structures and organizes the spaces we inhabit, establishing a platform of predictability in an otherwise chaotic sea of sensations and experiences.

Our bodies tell us the sizes of things; scale translates that to a different, more explicit form of knowing. A blister on a toe tells us we have walked too far; our smartphones tell us we've walked five miles. Both are indexes of scale, though one is tied diffusely to experience and the body while the other appeals more directly to our head in the form of a quantifiable known. We can feel lightness, smell rankness, taste bitterness, hear quietude, and see dimension. But we cannot know how big Earth is or how small a molecule is without measurement and scale. Scale itself, then, hovers in the space between the body and the brain, between percept and concept.

We do not come to scale naturally, as my daughter reminds me, we learn it. As a sixteen-year-old, working as a lifeguard at a youth summer camp, she would recount stories of little children who guessed that she was forty years old, or who begged to get under the sprinkler for fifteen minutes...but actually stayed for less than one. We do learn intellectually about measurement and scale in school, though that does not quite suffice to guide us through our everyday encounters. We form our innate understanding through physical experiences that are repeated across multiple contexts.

New York City overwhelms. Manhattan particularly. The building facades crowd out the sky. The noise and energy ricochets off the asphalt, concrete, limestone, and glassy walls...echoed and then amplified. Skyscrapers, tenements, high-rises, office buildings, and warehouses define the contours of our bodily experiences. And while these provide the containers for our lives, these aggregations of people and walls and spaces rarely ever reference the house or home as we have traditionally understood it. Human life is secondary to the infrastructure of this built colossus. When nature does make an appearance, whether as a weed in a crack in the sidewalk or as the mostly curated Central Park, it is only ever as a momentary distraction from the main event. It is a city whose logic, like that of Seoul or Hong Kong, is determined by the crane, the elevator, technology, steel, glass, and masonry. We may adapt or get used to the scale of a city, but that is simply another way of saying that its scale shapes us. We learn to habituate ourselves to the noise, we learn to sleep hundreds of feet up in the air, and we learn to become unruffled by sharing the sidewalk with thousands of people at once.

Fig. 6. *New York, New York.*

A walk down a street in Philadelphia is a very different experience. Three- and four-story homes predominate for as far as the eye can see. Known by many nicknames, including the "city of homes," Philadelphia, like San Francisco or Paris, was built to the scale of the human (and the horse), not the motorized crane. While Center City, the commercial and financial downtown, does sprout notable skyscrapers, they are anomalies, not the rule. They are more akin to Central Park—an oasis of otherness—than they are like Wall Street. The sky is accessible and available to the senses in Philadelphia. The height of most buildings is matched to the limits of human power, not to the possibilities of the crane and the elevator. Most people can walk up two or three flights of stairs. Manhattan is dense, thrusting upward; Philadelphia is horizontal, spreading gently outward. As in many global cities, its planners and architects and builders and inhabitants used human power and human capabilities to put it together. Certainly, human ingenuity overcame many physical limits, but the overall impression is one that fits the human eye. There is a complementary relationship between the human body, the built environment, and the kind of life that is possible to live here.

Concord, New Hampshire, is a large town in the guise of a capital city. It is entirely knowable, from east to west and from north to south. Hemmed in by forests and divided by the Merrimack River, its boundaries and its topography are conceptually graspable. No part of its entirety eludes the long-term resident's awareness. A bicyclist can navigate it all in a few hours, and a pedestrian can transverse it in a day. The gold-domed Capitol building—the tallest building in the town—glimmers in the northern sun, providing a fixed point of orientation. It is rational and knowable, scaled to the consciousness of its inhabitants.

Greensboro, Vermont, is of an entirely different order altogether. Here, nature is sovereign, and the human subject an afterthought. Situated in the Northeast Kingdom, as locals call this part of Vermont, it is a short drive to the Canadian border and worlds away from any urban agglomeration. Here, it is the human-built that is the exception. Frost heaves and water seeps. We are only guests here, and relentless natural forces eventually reclaim everything we build.

Fig. 7. *Greensboro, Vermont.*

Each environment establishes a very different set of relationships between the human body, human perception, human agency, and scale. The compression and the decompression, the noise and silence, the energy and struggle, exists in each...but exists in different ways in each. Katydids, chainsaws, and crazy loons break the quiet of northern Vermont; jackhammers, buses, and police sirens the nighttime peace of New York. But it is that other, perceptual realm that interests me here, that shadowy sense of measuring up to or against the environmental surround. Whether we are dwarfed by pine trees or skyscrapers, whether our vista opens up on a vast field of corn or an airshaft, these corporeal relations to scale shape the envelopes of our experience.

Scale is also the stuff of dreams and wonder. It has deep emotional resonance. The circus and the fairground use dramatic changes of size as techniques to lure us in, tempt our curiosity, and freak us out; everything is either bigger than life or smaller than life. Each wantonly plays to our childish fears and imaginations, as do children's books and movies. *Clifford the Big Red Dog*, *The Borrowers*, *The Big Friendly Giant*, *The Indian in the Cupboard*, *Gulliver's Travels*, *Fantastic Voyage*, *Honey I Shrunk the Kids*, *Downsized*, and *Ant-Man and the Wasp* all use outlandish shifts in scale to entangle us emotionally with things bigger and smaller than we are. These techniques target, not surprisingly, the developing scalar aptitudes of young children. Large and looming humans surround children, lumbering through their tiny worlds like species of an entirely different order. It's no surprise, then, that they are mesmerized by the juxtaposition and the transposition of big and small, mighty and vulnerable. This fascination with scale does not end with childhood, however. Contemporary artists as diverse as Claes Oldenburg and Coosje van Bruggen, Jeff Koons, Laurie Simmons, Tom Friedman, and Charles Ray plumb this same psychic terrain. Ray's *Family Romance* sculpture, for instance, scales up two toddlers to the size of their parents. The result: The age-appropriate proportions of the young children make them oddly monstrous at the scale of the adults, threatening the blissful "romance" of the nuclear family and reminding us that scale can also be home to a complex set of human emotions.

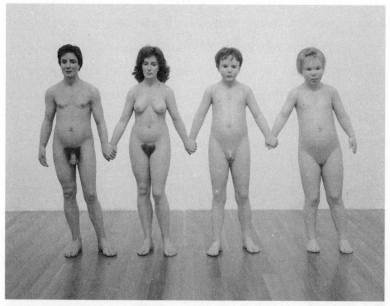

Fig. 8. *Charles Ray (b. 1953) © Copyright.* Family Romance. *1993. Painted fiberglass and synthetic hair, 53" x 7' l" x 11" (134.6 x 215.9 x 27.9 cm). Gift of The Norton Family. Courtesy Matthew Marks Gallery.*

The world does look different from the vantage of a young child: Giants actually do walk the earth, as do mammoth domesticated animals. Hours in the car seem to stretch on for days. A summer seems like forever to a three-year-old, as it comprises one-twelfth of her total life experience, but it goes by in the blink of an eye to her parent, who may be experiencing his fortieth. Our sense of scale, then, shifts over a lifetime, abetted by a combination of repeated experience and instruments of (imprecise) measure.

———

One way to understand more deeply the subtle dynamics of scale in relation to our sense of self and our surroundings is through concept of the figure/ground relationship. First identified by Gestalt psychologists at the end of the nineteenth century, the figure/ground relationship is an organizing principle of visual perception that is tied, in significant ways, to our capacity to adapt and survive. In any given scene, for example, we distinguish perceptually between the bounded (figure) and the boundless (ground); or between the discontinuous subject and the continuous background. A lion on

Fig. 9. *Figure (lightning) and ground (sky).*

the savannah is a figure against a ground. But when that lion crouches still, camouflaging itself in the grasses, the distinctions between figure and ground break down, creating a condition that makes our own survival less likely.

A figure, in this sense, can be a literal human figure, or it could be almost any object or perceptual discontinuity in the visual field, such as a vase or a tree or a car horn or even a filament of lightning against a foreboding sky. Figure 10 depicts a single figure against a ground of stairs and sky. In Agnes Martin's abstract modernist painting *The Tree*, on the other hand, spidery, uniform lines evenly divide up the negative space of the canvas, producing a significantly different perceptual experience. When the figure/ground distinction breaks down in a scene or in an image—when the figure disappears

Fig. 10. *A solitary figure against the ground of stairs and sky.*

or dissolves into the ground—our experience of the content of that image changes, as does our own bodily perception. Martin's gossamer gray grid resists our drive to find meaning, leaving us instead with only visual and spatial sensations.

Fig. 11. *Agnes Martin (1912–2004) © ARS, NY. The Tree. 1964. Oil and pencil on canvas, 6' x 6'. Larry Aldrich Foundation Fund. The Museum of Modem Art.*

We have learned to trust our eyes when it comes to photographic images, despite constant reminders that we are easily fooled. Both digital and analog images manipulate scale to draw us into their image space. Despite its realistic visual properties, the scene that a photograph depicts has no pregiven scale, and the edges of a photographic image, whether in printed form or on screen, establish no delimiting framework for the content inside of it. An eight-by-ten-inch photographic print can as easily contain an image of a city as it can the detailed surface of a microchip. We have come to rely upon the figure/ground relationships within that space to provide clues to what we are looking at.

The photograph below is, upon first inspection, a field of neutral gray, an almost pure field of visual sensation. Not only is it difficult to determine the content, but the scale is practically unknowable. In actuality, it is a photograph of fog over a lake, and so the scene is, in fact, vast.

Fig. 12. *Unstable figure/ground relationship.*

Because there is only continuous, nondistinct ground and no figure for us to anchor our gaze to, we lose the ability to figure out the scale of the image. We are lost in the collapse of figure and ground. A similar photograph, taken from the same vantage, reveals the blurry outlines of a fishing boat with two figures in it. Scale now snaps into place. We orient ourselves through the perceptual clues and situate our knowledge within the context of the image space. But is it really that simple? This certitude is built upon a foundation of trust that the hazy figural element in the image is, indeed, a full-scale boat and fisherman. It could, in fact, be a miniature cutout meant to deceive us.

Fig. 13. *A fishing boat (figure) emerges from the fog (ground).*

Photographers can easily manipulate this effect, as was the case in the famous photograph of the bustling crowd assembled around the statue of Saddam Hussein in Firdos Square in Baghdad when the U.S. forces dragged the statue to the ground in 2003. The photographs that circulated immediately after the event showed a huge crowd gathered, reinforcing the U.S. military's contention that throngs of Iraqis were there to celebrate the overthrow of the dictator. But that was only because the photographer had established the image frame closely cropped to the dozens of spectators that were assembled there. Later, images that were less closely cropped showed a large plaza with only a smattering of people, undercutting the United States' strategic contention that the overthrow was wildly popular.

Cognitively, we anchor our perception of scale in a photographic image through its association with figural elements whose scale we know from experience. Or think we do. Online retailer Amazon.com, which has typically communicated the physical characteristics of its books by providing an unscaled, cropped image of the book cover, recently started providing scalar clues tied to the human figure. The shadowy gray figure emerges from the white ground while, ironically, the book takes its place as a figure against the ground of human body.

A photograph is a concentrated form that aims to capture the essence of the world that exists around us, albeit at a scale that is, by degrees, less than the world itself. For instance, we "read" the photographic representation of the fisherman in Figure 13 almost as if we're looking out a small window at it, even though the photograph is, itself, a reduction in size of a scene that we reimagine in our mind's eye at full scale. When we hold an eight-by-ten-inch photograph of a city skyline in

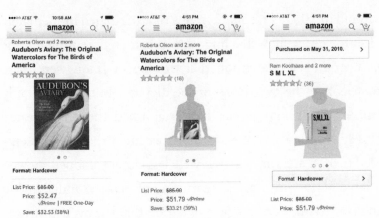

Fig. 14. *Using the human figure for scale on Amazon.com.*

our hands, we conveniently overlook the fact that we cannot hold a city in our hands. We have been conditioned to ignore the fact that qualities such as size, focus, resolution, dynamic range, perspective, and proportion are the artifacts of a photographic lens and sensor and not our eye. A photograph thus acts as a kind of visual scale model of the scene itself, though by now we pay scant attention to that conceptual slippage. We no longer seem to "see" scale in the photographic image.

———

In March 2016, a company named Surrey NanoSystems announced an audacious innovation. Surrey NanoSystems, to that point in history, was best known for the creation of Vantablack, a material so dark that it absorbed all but 0.035 percent of visible light. In other words, a material so black that it is almost unseeable. Their announcement, in 2016, was that they had just pulled out of their reactor a new, even blacker material. How much blacker? The spectrometers they used to measure reflected light could detect no light bouncing off of it. It essentially broke their instruments.[2] The inventors of Vantablack, in describing its optical properties, suggest that "it could be said that it is almost impossible to 'see' Vantablack as so little light is reflected from the surface. However, the observer's brain of course tries to make sense of what it is seeing, with the result that some people describe it like looking into a hole!"[3] And this is a reaction to the first version of Vantablack, not the more recent material that effectively evaded their sophisticated instrumentation.

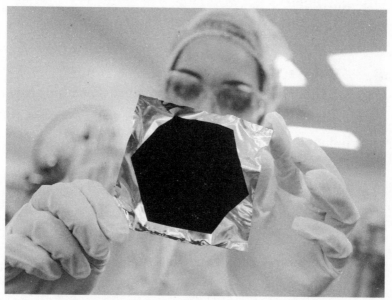

Fig. 15. *Vantablack sample, © Surrey NanoSystems.*

Not a pigment, or a color, this "functionalised 'forest' of millions upon millions of incredibly small tubes made of carbon, or carbon nanotubes" was eventually classified in the UK as a "dual use" material, in part because of its "performance beyond the visible spectrum." Because the UK labeled the material as dual use—having both civilian and military applications—they could regulate and restrict its use and export. Surrey NanoSystems then took the unlikely step of restricting its creative use to one single artist, Anish Kapoor. They chose to "license Vantablack S-VIS exclusively to Kapoor Studios UK to explore its use in works of art. This exclusive license limits the coating's use in the field of art, but does not extend to any other sectors."[4] Kapoor, a globetrotting, high-profile sculptor of large-scale works, saw a unique potential for this extreme material. For him, the appeal was somatic. "It's effectively like a paint.... Imagine a space that's so dark that as you walk in you lose all sense of where you are, what you are, and especially all sense of time. Something happens to your emotional self and in disorientation one has to reach in for other resources."[5]

Beyond the ability of sensitive instruments to measure, Vantablack provokes perceptual hiccups: It defies vision like a black hole and, according to Kapoor, it existentially disorients the human subject in space and time. Figure and ground merge while space and time collapse. Pushed to an extreme, the material evidences the disorienting logic of scalar change, producing unsettling and unexpected results. Instruments fail, the eye misrecognizes, and the brain is baffled. Scale is directly tied to our emotional states. Without something knowable to push against, we risk losing ourselves in the void.

What sense of scale are we learning when we peer into our computer screens, our smartphones, and tablets? How are its laws of physics remaking ours? Against what ground are we figuring ourselves out? The industrial age brought to us a new sense of figure/ground relations, and we evolved through that entanglement. The information age is delivering an entirely new set of experiences. Recent Nielsen research reveals that adult Americans now spend nearly five hours per day in front of digital screens (and close to twelve hours a day engaged with media, if you include television and radio).[6] How can we imagine that this monumental shift in our daily habits won't also change us somehow? The space behind the screen is already a quixotic wonderland of signals, transistors, information, and pixels that combine together to create a tantalizing alternative to our humdrum everyday. What new world will we be immersing ourselves in when we slip on our virtual reality goggles? Space, in virtual reality, is both dimensional and impossible. It is a set of visual cues that the designer mobilizes to build an illusion that tricks our body, our brain, and our senses (though, for now, mostly visual and some tactile). In virtual reality, we may be able to dance on the head of a pin and float in the space between electrons. We will have the potential to even more fully remake scale in this fully digital environment. As such, we will also have the capacity to fully remake ourselves. Perhaps we will look out into the void of this new virtual space and see not emptiness, but Vantablack.

Chapter 03

These Go to 11

In the summer of 2009, eight years after the attacks of September 11, the United States was still entangled militarily in Afghanistan and Iraq. The incursions, which were meant to be swift deployments of overwhelming military force, were instead becoming quagmires. In this context, Elisabeth Bumiller of the *New York Times* reported on a briefing in Kabul, Afghanistan, that had reached Dr. Strangelove–like proportions.

General Stanley McChrystal, the leader of U.S. and NATO forces at that time, was sitting down to a PowerPoint briefing that included a slide that his analysts had created to represent—in one diagram—the dynamics of the counterinsurgency effort. Faced with an impenetrably dense and tangled diagram, which Bumiller described as "a bowl of spaghetti," General McChrystal famously quipped, "When we understand that slide, we'll have won the war." The room, according to sources, "erupted in laughter."

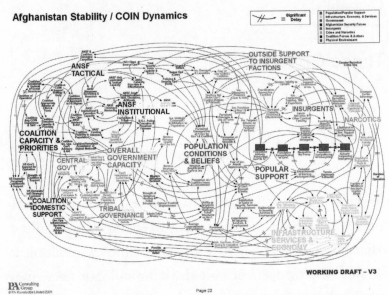

Fig. 16. *Afghanistan Stability/COIN Dynamics—Security, 2009. Public document from the Office of the United States Joint Chiefs of Staff.*

Something very strange was going on in that moment. A subtle and nearly imperceptible force was remapping his operational theater, forcing him to confront a confounding reality that still haunts us years later. The map—or in this case the diagram—had exceeded the territory, so to speak. Logistical coordination was proving more confounding than Afghani military resistance. McChrystal's team's ability to amass and represent intelligence and interconnectedness had outstripped its capacity to act effectively on it. It was not as if overwhelming military force had, in some magical way, become impossible. It was as if, instead, the *quantity* of data available had altered the very *quality* of the information. Scale had transformed signal into noise.

While Bumiller's article focuses on the dangers of Power-Point as an information delivery channel, McChrystal's wry quip, however, is clearly targeted at the nature of the information graphic itself. The diagram is not without thoughtful insights, and few would argue that the situation on the ground in Afghanistan was not infernally complicated. The sum in this case, however, is so massively greater than the parts that the overall diagram is operationally useless, or at least that's what McChrystal's remark implies. The level of detail of the diagram's nodes and connections swells our cognitive load to the point of breaking. It is too much to take in. And the vagueness of the arrows of causality or force deflect deep analytical insight. It is both too specific and too general at the same time.

"When we understand that slide, we'll have won the war." General McChrystal's comment about the state of play in twenty-first-century warfare eerily reflects a characteristic of systems as they change in scale. In this case, the information, the connections, and the nodes in the diagram had multiplied so rapidly in number that the "problem" had fundamentally changed. The absurd irony that General McChrystal points out is that, in their aspiration to map everything, the "Afghanistan Stability: COIN Dynamics" diagram's designers fundamentally changed the problem. Strategically (and from an information designer's point of view), the aim of an exercise like that would be to reduce the complexity down to a scale where a new possibility reveals itself. What the diagram makers did not account for in the nature of systems is that as they grow and change in scale they can suddenly shape-shift: The slide becomes the war and logistics becomes the enemy.

Artifacts and systems that change in scale can surprise us, confounding our ability to predict their behaviors. These unanticipated swerves in outcomes explain, in part, why we struggle to make sense of things at a time when the volume of things we routinely encounter (millions of files, billions of people, trillions of dollars) is so rapidly increasing. When systems evolve from linear and predictable in growth to nonlinear and unpredictable, our capacity to comprehend our own context quickly becomes unsettled.

———

In 1968 the Austrian plant biologist Frits Went published a thought experiment involving ants, humans, and the effects of shifting scale. In an *American Scientist* article titled "The Size of Man," he explored the fascinating relationship between scale and behavior, contrasting the physical possibilities afforded by the microworld of the ant and the macroworld of the human. The safe assumption would be that the rules of the physical apply in just the same way to an ant as they do to a human, just scaled down proportionally. Went, however, demonstrates just how wrongheaded that thinking is.

Can an ant learn to read? The answer to that question might seem to hinge on whether or not you believe that ants have enough intellectual capacity to learn a complex skill like reading. Ants are, of course, relatively simple at the individual level, but they show surprising behaviors at the level of the colony. But that, in fact, is not the issue. According to Went, the problem is one of scale. As a book shrinks down to a size that an ant could read, the molecular bonds between the pages become so strong relative to the ant that it would be impossible for an ant to turn the pages. In other words, as you change scale, the problem changes. Moreover, Went continues, "decreasing letter size a thousandfold would bring them to the limits of visibility since visible light cannot resolve shapes under 1μ. If ants wanted mechanically to record information they would have to use tablets like the Assyrians. Yet, they would be unable to chisel characters into stone surfaces because, at their size, hammers are ineffective, packing hardly any kinetic energy."[1]

At the scale of an ant, water droplets cannot wash away the dirt on the ant's exoskeleton because the surface tension of water is so strong that a drop of water will simply bounce off of the ant. Instead, each ant leg has small hooks and barbs used both to climb and to scrape off dirt and other substances. And on and on Went goes: Ants cannot enjoy a cup of coffee (the surface tension is too great to pour liquids) or a cigarette (flame does not scale down in size and the ant cannot get close enough to the flame) or wear clothing (the forces of adhesion would make removing the clothes impossible). Went's point, overall, is that the laws of physics determine different possibilities at different scales, dependent upon the organism's relative size. All organisms, he suggests, are limited in their capabilities by the ratio of their size to their mass, and the capacity of living things to operate in the world is functionally dependent upon scale. "If man were twice as tall as he is now, his kinetic energy in falling would be so great (32 times more than at normal size), that it would not be safe for him to walk upright."[2] He makes the additional argument that one must reconsider the kinds of physical laws that apply at differing scales. The human, according to Went, exists in the realm of classical mechanics—that is, the laws of Isaac Newton. At this scale, bodies experience physical effects that depend, primarily, on the laws of gravity. The ant, conversely, is more influenced by molecular and thermodynamic properties, which differ in dramatic ways from Newtonian forces. Even measuring length and mass becomes unstable at the scale of an ant. Went's thought experiments demonstrate that a shift in scales can result in surprising outcomes. Physicists refer to this phenomenon—the instances where system behaviors change as the scale changes—as *scalar variance* or *scalar asymmetry*.

———

How radical can these phase changes be? Let's consider the metamorphosis of the butterfly. What happens in that black box of the chrysalis or the cocoon? When a pupa is cut open in midcourse, what is visible to the naked eye is not a caterpillar, not a butterfly, not some curious hybrid of the two, but simply goo.[3] In the life cycle of organisms like caterpillars, which are actually larvae, they start to grow and eat and grow and eat until they reach a certain, genetically determined size and mass. That is, they grow in a predictable, linear way. But once they reach that predetermined threshold, hormones start pumping, genes turn on, and an unprecedented phase change commences. The process starts when the caterpillar attaches itself upside down to a surface, often a leaf, and then either spins a cocoon or molts to form a chrysalis. Once encapsulated, the caterpillar releases an enzyme that dissolves its own tissues and its organs, turning from a solid creature into liquid goo. Floating about in the goo, however, are some remarkable bits called imaginal discs, small aggregations of rapidly dividing cells that provide a proto-structure for wings, antennae, legs, eyes, genitals, and other constituent parts of the adult butterfly.

With her research collaborators, biologist Martha Weiss revealed a stunning facet of this already miraculous transmutation. She and her team tested the neural persistence of conditioned responses to negative stimuli. In other words, they exposed caterpillars to a foul-smelling odor, ethyl acetate, and as they did so they also buzzed them with a mild electric shock to negatively condition them. Significantly, the caterpillars did learn from the exposure. In a test in which they had the choice between a chamber with no aroma and one with ethyl acetate, a very high proportion of the caterpillars

(78 percent) sought out the stink-free chamber. After metamorphosis, the researchers tested the butterflies with the same choice, giving them the option between a chamber with the foul aroma (negatively associated with electrical shock) or no aroma, and the butterflies chose the non-ethyl acetate chamber at almost exactly the same high rate (77 percent) as when they were caterpillars. Somehow, despite melting itself down to goo during metamorphosis, the caterpillar's memories persisted.[4]

While the persistence of memories in holometabolous organisms (that is, organisms that go through metamorphic changes) is indeed remarkable, it is overshadowed by the radical transformation that happens at the macro level. What was once a creeping, leaf-chomping, gravitationally challenged caterpillar emerges as a dancing, nectar-sipping spirit of the air. Somehow, the cells that were programmed in the larva to become one type of organism contain the programming that enables the larva to dissolve itself down to almost nothing and reconstitute itself as a whole new type of being. As the scale changes, the system behaviors change. What starts out as a caterpillar fundamentally transforms, with the addition of food and some genetic triggers, into an organism that bears little resemblance to its original self, though its sensate memories do, miraculously, persist. Both the ant and the butterfly reveal the vicissitudes of scale: As systems or elements within systems change in scale, the nature of their reality shifts in unpredictable ways.

If we move even further down in scale than the caterpillar and the ant, the behavior of matter becomes even more astonishing. Superposition, a principle of physics at the quantum level, suggests that at certain orders of magnitude—specifically, the quantum level—particles can be in two places at the same time or share their states across a distance. (It is an astounding, even mind-bending finding, frankly... though not a very new one.) Since at least the 1930s, scientists have posited that as we move down in scale to the quantum level, things should behave in some very strange ways. Unconvinced, Albert Einstein disparagingly called this hypothesis "spooky action at a distance," although more recent discoveries have proved Einstein wrong. These odd behaviors happen only, however, once we slide down the scale of perception to the nearly invisible and the hardly imaginable. Jim Al-Khalili and Johnjoe McFadden, two science writers who explore not just the world of quantum mechanics (how quantum phenomena affect energy and matter in our physical world) but also the emerging field of quantum biology (how these same phenomena affect living systems at the cellular level), describe the conundrum this way:

> If quantum mechanics can so beautifully and accurately describe the behaviour of atoms with all their accompanying weirdness, then why aren't all the objects we see around us, including us—which are after all only made up of these atoms—also able to

be in two places at once, pass through impenetrable barriers or communicate instantaneously across space? One obvious difference is that the quantum rules apply to single particles or systems consisting of just a handful of atoms, whereas much larger objects consist of trillions of atoms bound together in mindboggling variety and complexity. Somehow, in ways we are only now beginning to understand, most of the quantum weirdness washes away ever more quickly the bigger the system is, until we end up with the everyday objects that obey the familiar rules of what physicists call the "classical world."[5]

Humans, it seems, are just too big, messy, and complex to delight in the curious rules at the quantum scale. But while we may not be able to enjoy the benefits of quantum superposition, that isn't necessarily true for other living creatures. Tongcang Li and Zhang-Qi Yin have recently proposed to molecularly adhere a bacterium to an aluminum membrane in order to see what happens when this assemblage is brought to a state of quantum superposition. Researchers at the University of Colorado have already put the aluminum membrane into a quantum state. The microorganism is considerably smaller than the aluminum membrane, and so for this next experiment their hope is that they will be able to record what happens to living matter when it is subjected to the mysteries of quantum forces.[6] *Entanglement* is the word that quantum physicists use to describe the improbable condition of a particle maintaining a physical relationship with its quantum double, and there are few words better to describe our complex, evolving relationship to scale. What is impossible at the scale of the mountain, the tree, the elephant, the bear, the human, the cat, the flea, or even the dust mite is, in fact, imaginable and even empirically testable at the scale of a simple bacterium.

———

The things we encounter in the world, whether they are physical artifacts (dust or mountains), immaterial forces (wind or light), or even concepts (problems or opportunities) come in all sorts of sizes. We perceive, for instance, that pressure at work is mounting, or is even overwhelming. We have built an internal instrument of sorts that helps us to evaluate relative degrees of its presence in our everyday experience in a way that is analogous to measuring a change in temperature in the air outside our window or the pressure within our automobile tires. Apparently, we are able to sense this insensible pressure increasing, decreasing, and changing in scale. But the things we encounter perceptually do not always obey regular rules and laws as their scalar frames shift, especially as we encounter a more digitally mediated world.

If, for example, I open a document in the popular word processing application Microsoft Word, I have the option to set the size of the page that I will work on. Let's say I set it to a standard U.S. *letter* size, 8.5 by 11 inches. That way, anything that I write will be formatted to fit onto an 8.5" × 11" sheet of paper, just as it appears on my screen. This innovation—WYSIWYG, or "what you see is what you get"—made computers much more accessible to novice users and built a stronger bridge between the digital world and our physical world as we know it. Microsoft Word also lets me view the document on my screen at a variety of magnifications, ranging from 10 percent to 500 percent, so that I can zoom in and see the type forms and spacing close up, or I can zoom out and see what the whole page might look like once it's printed. It's a simple but effective feature of the software application, and it allows the user to work on the document at a comfortable and familiar distance. If I decide to view my 8.5" × 11" document at 100 percent magnification, how large is the document that I'm viewing on my screen? The obvious answer would be that 100 percent of 8.5 by 11 inches is 8.5 by 11 inches. And yet, if I take out my ruler and measure the "document" window that I see on my fifteen-inch laptop computer screen, I discover in this world of the computer desktop that 100 percent of 8.5 by 11 inches is actually 6.25 by 8.125 inches. And to make matters even more confusing, this measurement of 100 percent of an 8.5" × 11" document will likely vary across computer monitors depending upon their respective sizes and resolutions. While this is a shift of miniscule significance, something has slipped in our relation to scale that is rewriting our perceptual universe, albeit in relatively unremarkable and insignificant ways.

These same sorts of scalar entanglements of perception are a common occurrence for those who work frequently editing images in a desktop environment. Anybody could tell you that the two images of mushrooms in Figure 17 are identical. Even looked at up close there is no discernable difference. And yet, the image on the left is 600 by 600 pixels small, and the one on the right is 2,544 by 2,544 pixels large. To our senses, in the visual space of the computer-mediated environment, they are identical. Printed to their actual size, one is not much larger than a postage stamp and the other is the size of a small poster.

Fig. 17. *Two seemingly identical images that differ significantly in pixel scale.*

There is a fundamental perceptual gap between the image space on-screen and that in real life—just as in the case of the MS Word document. Designers who work on computers struggle with this all the time. When designing a poster, for instance, it is one thing to get the proportions worked out in the document that exists on-screen, but it's something very different when that same file is printed out and put on the wall. Even though the page layout application shrinks the file down proportionally on the screen (that is, by linear increments), maintaining all ratios and relationships, the eye perceives something qualitatively different when the document is at full scale and available to our sense in the physical realm. In each of these examples—the MS Word document that isn't what it says it is and the Photoshop images that can be the same and different at the same time—we see that a computer-mediated environment has fundamentally altered the perceptual cues that undergird our everyday experience. The distortions in these instances are hardly life altering, but they do point to a subtle shift that is taking place in our perceptual capacity as we spend more and more time in the hybrid space between bits and atoms.

———

Digital immateriality does not just affect our sensory perception of the things around us. It also changes how our economies create and circulate value. If economics is war by other means, then the radical asymmetries and aproportionalities that are appearing on the emerging electronic battlefields will just as likely show up in the digital marketplace: The insignificant will become unimaginably all-powerful and the value-less valuable. In 2010 Chris Anderson, former editor in chief of *Wired* magazine, published a book titled *Free: How Today's Smartest Businesses Profit by Giving Something for Nothing.* The book traces the development of a relatively new kind of economic condition, one fashioned by the rise of information networks and the easy reproducibility of digital "things." Anderson builds upon *Moore's law*—the projection that processing speed would double every two years—suggesting that innovation in technical capacity is also driving down costs in all three of the main drivers of the digital economy: processing power, bandwidth, and digital storage. In fact, they are dropping so precipitously that they are pushing down the costs to make, distribute, and store digital goods to close to nothing…or, in some cases, nothing itself. Whether or not the costs are actually zero, they are close enough to zero to make them negligible. This near-infinite supply has the effect of upending many of the tenets of business strategy. Companies can offer goods and services for nearly free and yet generate tremendous value through the volume of traffic and data that they can collect from the many users.

Free, as Anderson points out, has a history. Parking at supermarkets is free. Many mobile phone companies give away their phones for free. But in each of these cases, cross-subsidies are bearing the costs of free: food prices are higher to pay for parking; the costs of the mobile phones are amortized across the phone's carriage contract. Radio and television services for most of the twentieth century were free to the public on the airwaves, and yet it was advertisers and their third-party clients that paid for the free service. Consumers wouldn't necessarily see that the cost of advertising was actually built into the additional cost of the products (to pay for the adverts to pay for the free radio). But as Anderson points out, free in the world of electronic bits is a species totally different from free in the marketplace of atoms.[7]

Google, for instance, gives away a huge raft of goods and services—from search to word processing and email platforms to YouTube content and image storage—asking for nothing in return. But it has found ways—more or less inventing the click-through ad format—to bring advertisers in as a third party to sell ad space to Google's users. Google has built a multi-billion-dollar company while charging its consumers nothing for its services, a remarkable example of an economy tipped on its head. They have monetized attention. In creating such incredibly popular services, Google also makes money off the data they scrape from the users themselves. Google outsmarted its rivals, Anderson suggests, by creating a search algorithm that performed better as the web increased in size, whereas their competitors faced increasing costs with increasing usage. The company was able to scale to the size of its user base without increasing costs significantly—and by generating revenue in other ways. "Where abundance drives the costs of something to the floor," Anderson writes, "value shifts to adjacent levels."[8]

In one example he cites, the alternative band Radiohead decided to abandon traditional avenues for selling their music and dip their toes into the waters of the "free" economy, also, albeit in novel ways. Rather than go through the usual retail and distribution channels, Radiohead opted to sell directly to its fans on the internet. Anybody could download their album *In Rainbows* and pay nothing, if that struck them as fair, or pay what they felt they ought to pay for the new content. The cost to reproduce the digital file was next to nothing, unlike traditional pressings of vinyl or writing of compact discs, so their only true cost was in bandwidth, storage, and cost of hosting the FTP site for the album, all of which add up to very little. *In Rainbows*, as a result, became Radiohead's most commercially successful album, moving more than 3 million copies, and they made more money from digital downloads of their albums than they had from any of their previous, more conventional releases.[9]

In these instances, increases or decreases in scale do not simply enlarge or shrink the economies proportionally, but they rewrite the rules entirely. While in the cases of both Google and Radiohead, however, money does change hands, whether through the third-party approach (Google's ad sense) or through a pay-what-you-will sense of honor/guilt with Radiohead. Google still found a way to create value by giving away their products.

Wikipedia, though, is a different economic story. Built entirely through the efforts of energetic and dedicated volunteers, Wikipedia marshaled unparalleled quantities of free labor to build a category-killing free encyclopedia. Why would thousands of unpaid laborers donate their time, energy, and wisdom to build a product that has no real precedent? Anderson suggests that there are two forces at play in the meteoric rise and sustained success of Wikipedia. First of all, the volunteer labor does provide value to its donors, but not in monetary ways. Instead, they generate boosts to their own sense of self through the three vectors of community, personal growth, and discharging their own cognitive surplus. In other words, they are likely not fully challenged by the work that their bosses ask them to do (they have a cognitive surplus), they learn something about a topic that interests them by writing and wrangling about it (personal growth), and their standing within a community skyrockets as a result of their efforts (community). Whether these are fans of Judy Garland, collectors of LED Casio watches, or voices looking to shape how history views the U.S. invasions of Iraq, their labor produces value, just not economic value as we have known it.

The second force that helps to explain Wikipedia's success is directly attributable to its scale: Because it is so large, only a tiny percentage of its users need to contribute in order for it to be successful. Here again, the increasing scale of the user base generates new forms in the value chain. Anderson estimates that about one in ten thousand readers of the online encyclopedia contribute as authors, but because it is globally distributed and free to all, its user base is astronomically large. A tiny percentage of a huge number can be a surprisingly large number.[10] Anderson admonishes his readers not to think in terms of scarcity—as classical economics theory suggests—but instead in terms of a new economy of abundance that the internet has spawned. When things are free, as he repeats, new value emerges elsewhere. In other words, as scale changes, the problem or opportunity changes. The spoils, in these cases, accrue to those who are clever enough to anticipate where that new value will pop up, and to be there first.

In an effort to capitalize on the principles he was describing, Anderson convinced the book's publisher to follow him down the path to free. Following the internet publisher Tim O'Reilly's adage that "the enemy of the author is not piracy, but obscurity," he inspired his publisher to develop a publishing strategy that followed the rules that he himself observed about this strange new economy.[11] When the book launched, it was possible to read the entire book for free on Scribd and at Google Books. The entire book was not available to download or to print, though a nine-page excerpt was. And, in a strange twist, one could download the entire audiobook, but if you wanted to download the abridged audiobook, it cost $7.49.[12] Here we have reached the foggy bottom of scalar effects on pricing, value, and content on the internet. The economy of abundance has so disfigured classical economics that Anderson and his publisher are twisting their price tiers into pretzels trying to figure out where value will pop its head up next. Undoubtedly, there are some time-is-money calculations—the abridged audiobook costs more than the free one—and the publisher also only offered some of these free versions for a limited time to create buzz. But what is also quite apparent is that the massive scale of networks and plummeting costs of production, distribution, and storage are wreaking havoc on value as we know it.[13]

———

How did data become big? We encounter this same system-level "phase change" in the realm of data, and here again changes in scale create unpredictable new forms—in this case, of knowledge, insight, and control. *Big data* is a description of scale, certainly. The evolution of *data* into *big data* tracks a shift from one quality of information to another, or so the apostles of big data would have us believe.

In the eyes of its beholders, big data is more than just more data. Most of us think of the company Amazon as a seller of goods: from toiletries and toys to chainsaws and grapefruits. They expanded their services from selling products to producing original, streaming television content from their site, and they also started designing and manufacturing smartphones and tablets and e-book readers. For much of its history Amazon has been unprofitable, despite dominating the landscape of digital distribution in a way that rivals brick-and-mortar stores such as Walmart, and Sears Roebuck and Co. before that. However, along the way, Amazon recognized that while it might lose money or barely break even from its retail business, there were other fish to fry financially. As of October 2015, Amazon Web Services made up 8 percent of

Amazon's revenue but an eye-popping 52 percent of its operating profit, and profit from its cloud business outpaced profit from the rest of the company's departments combined.[14] In other words, Amazon's fastest-growing and most profitable component is the provision of web server capacity and business infrastructure—not delivering diapers by drone. Amazon recognized that storage and data management was a key service in a data-driven economy, and they positioned themselves early on to be a leader in that field, building massive server farms across the world, often in remote, cold climates (the servers generate tremendous amounts of heat, so locating them in chilly climates reduces costs). Their reason for building their business this way goes to the heart of scalar changes in data culture and management.

New forms of value, in the end, is what distinguishes data from big data. That value can come in the form of economic return, insights, better services, higher personalization, or closer surveillance, as we have come to learn. Netflix, for instance, the company that once had a core business of mailing DVDs to subscribers' homes, recognized that they also had a trove of information about the likes and dislikes of its users, with information as detailed as what its viewers paused on, rewound, fast-forwarded through, or gave up on watching. With the knowledge they gleaned from roughly thirty million "plays" a day, Netflix hatched *House of Cards*, a highly successful streaming series based on three very well known (from their data), successful quantities: the director David

Fincher, the actor Kevin Spacey, and the British political drama *House of Cards*. Netflix triangulated the data to predict, in a sense, the future success of its content, or at least to limit its risk. Their data analysts knew intimately what Netflix's subscribers liked and didn't like, though in this case it was not based upon their avowed preferences, but upon the mass aggregation of actual and unconscious behaviors.

Big data, and the culture around it, is still only in its toddler stage, with growing pains and stumbles to follow. For instance, as part of an emerging fitness culture, many people started to wear fitness tracking bands around their wrists, logging their steps and heart rates and other personal health data. Many of these same wearers were also runners who belonged to a digital service, called Strava, that maps and aggregates runs for the fitness community. Using Strava, one can save both a map of a run and the data associated with it (heart rate, path, duration of run, elevation change, and so on). When those maps are published to Strava by the community, one can identify new places to run at home or best routes to run while traveling to foreign cities. In 2017, Strava decided to publish a "heatmap" of all the routes its athletes had mapped while using its application, opening its treasure trove of information to users and application developers in the hope of sparking further innovation in the product and service ecosystem. As they announced, "this update includes six times more data than before—in total 1 billion activities from all Strava data through September 2017. Our global heatmap is the largest, richest, and most beautiful dataset of its kind. It is a direct visualization of Strava's global network of athletes." What they did not anticipate was that opening up their data to a broader community would create a national security incident. Tracking and aggregating health data seemed like such a good idea, it turned out, that the U.S. Army had also equipped some of its service women and men with fitness trackers, hoping to monitor and, ultimately, improve the overall health of its millions of soldiers. In documenting *all* its users on the global "heatmap," Strava inadvertently revealed both the activity within and the location of sensitive and even secret U.S. military bases.[15] To make matters worse, it was even possible to track individual paths of movement back to specific, identified individuals. While some U.S. military bases were already known or findable on Google's or Apple's map applications, not all were. In Afghanistan, for instance, a secret "base itself is not visible on the satellite views of commercial providers such as Google Maps or Apple's Maps, yet it can be clearly seen through Strava." Typically, because soldiers were limited to exercising on the base itself, the boundaries of the base were etched as a bright line as the runners circumnavigated the base's perimeter in search of the most unfettered runs. As a result of this breach, the U.S. military has had to, yet again, rethink its policy around data privacy and soldiers' activity trackers, tablets, computers, and smartphones, just as it did when its recruits revealed sensitive location data while playing Pokémon Go, enlisting in Foursquare, or having sensitive conversations in front of "smart" television sets (that could monitor their conversations).[16] Few could have foreseen that a fitness tracker could, when aggregated together with millions of others, phase-change into a tool for espionage.

What makes big data "large, rich, and beautiful"? There are myriad definitions for it, and together they reveal something unexpected about the phenomenon. For many, the first appearance of the idea of big data came about because of a simple issue of linear scale. Data scientists joke that big data is data that is so voluminous that it breaks Excel. That is, the size of relational databases and the need to aggregate, store, and analyze the data overflowing Excel spreadsheets had rendered the software unequal to the task. In 2001, well before the term came into popular use, Doug Laney, a data management analyst, coined his "3V" framework that many still use today to describe an emerging confluence of data vectors: volume, velocity, and variety.[17] Responding to the increase in electronic commerce and data storage, Laney accurately diagnosed the conditions that would lead to the explosion in data—greater volume, coming in at a much faster rate, and from databases that do not share a common format or semantic structure. Later, in 2011, the market intelligence firm IDC would amend Laney's characterization, inserting "value" as a fourth V in the framework: "Big data technologies describe a new generation of technologies and architectures, designed to economically extract value from very large volumes of a wide variety of data, by enabling high-velocity capture, discovery, and/or analysis."[18] In this conception, value becomes the mysterious supplement that emerges from the bigness... from the scalar phase change.

Not all data scientists agree on what the *big* in *big data* actually refers to. In 2014, at the height of big data mania, Jennifer Dutcher, a community relations manager for the data science program at the University of California, Berkeley, published online a survey of forty influential data scientists, managers, and writers. She simply asked them to define *big data*. What she got in return was a kaleidoscopic vantage on what *big* might mean (emphases in the original):

- Big data means *data that cannot fit easily into a standard relational database* (Hal Varian).
- *The term big data is really only useful if it describes a quantity of data that's so large that traditional approaches to data analysis are doomed to failure.* That can mean that you're doing complex analytics on data that's too large to fit into memory or it can mean that you're dealing with a data storage system that doesn't offer the full functionality of a standard relational database. What's essential is that your old way of doing things doesn't apply anymore and can't just "be scaled out" (John Myles White).
- Everything we know spits out data today—not just the devices we use for computing. We now get digital exhaust from our garage door openers to our coffee pots, and everything in between. At the same time,

we have become a generation of people who demand instantaneous access to information—from what the weather is like in a country thousands of miles away to which store has better deals on toaster ovens. *Big data is at the intersection of collecting, organizing, storing, and turning all of that raw data into truly meaningful information* (Prakash Nanduri).

- *Big data is not all about volume, it is more about combining different data sets and to analyze it in real-time to get insights for your organization.* Therefore, the right definition of Big Data should in fact be: Mixed Data (Mark van Rijmenam).
- Big data: *Endless possibilities or cradle-to-grave shackles, depending upon the political, ethical, and legal choices we make* (Deirdre Mulligan).
- Big data, which started as a technological innovation in distributed computing, is now *a cultural movement by which we continue to discover how humanity interacts with the world*—and each other—at large-scale (Drew Conway).
- For me, the technological definitions (like "too big to fit in an Excel spreadsheet" or "too big to hold in memory") are important, but aren't really the main point. *Big data for me is data at a scale and scope that changes in some fundamental way (not just at the margins) the range of solutions that can be considered when people and organizations face a complex problem.* Different solutions, not just "more, better" (Steven Weber).[19]

What Steven Weber describes—not just more, better—is the phase change through which quantitative shifts become qualitative transformations. Water becomes a vapor, data becomes value. What is evident across these definitions is that bigness is hardly a quantitative matter. Instead, for some of the scientists, it is an index for something different, not something larger. If regular-sized data tells us what we already know, the dream of big data is that it can provide an X-ray into our patterns of decision-making, selection, and behavior that we cannot see by other means, that it will reveal ourselves to ourselves in much the same way that Freud's discovery of the unconscious uncovered a deeper truth about who we are and ushered us into a modern era of subjective self-reflection. Metadata becomes metaphysics.

———

What is tantalizing, or terrifying, about big data is the promise that something new and unexpected will emerge when data scientists bring heavy processing power to bear upon massive quantities of data. These modern data miners will extract the digital equivalent of gold, bauxite, or tantalum from our everyday behaviors when we're not even paying attention.

From an analytical standpoint, the amassing of data in quantities that qualify as big represents a tectonic shift in the way we glean insight from data itself. We have been producing and collecting digital data for close to a half century now, so data collection is not a new phenomenon. In the early days of computing, most data was structured, meaning that it was preformatted and organized into discrete units that had an order to them. Analysts could search the data by key terms, as well, in order to sort and filter the data into meaningful subunits. Spreadsheets and databases, the unseen understructure of the computing world, comprised the organizational matrix for data production and consumption. We call information structured, when, for instance, an analyst can effectively create a relatively simple query that can aggregate, read, and analyze the data without missing out on vast quantities of important material. A tax return is structured data, as is a bead store's inventory, even though it may have millions of beads fitting into thousands of categories. The combined inventories of beads from a hundred bead stores in a franchise represents massive data, yet it is still structured data. Structure does not relate to the size of the data pool, only to its organization. Today, much of the data that comprises our digital culture is still structured, it's just that its mass is dwarfed by the metastasizing swelling of unstructured data.

Unstructured data is the holy grail of data analytics, however, as it represents a massive resource just waiting to be mined. A digital photograph, for instance, is unstructured data. As are the contents of word processing files, tweets, blog posts, audio files, and digital videos. There are estimates that up to 90 percent of the content on the internet is currently unstructured data, which is why so many are trying to find ways to mine it more effectively. A digital photo one posts to a social media site, for instance, will automatically generate a certain amount of structured data that a company can profitably mine: the name of the account that posted it, the time it was posted, the date, any hashtags posted with it, other accounts that "liked" it, as well as its metadata. But what most companies cannot automatically discern is the actual content of the image. Its array of pixels may have an organization to it, but there is nothing inherent to that organization of the array that reveals whether the photo contains an eggplant, an onion, or a skyscraper.

Consider a video of a teenage girl doing a skateboard trick that she and her friends post to a social media site and tag with the hashtag #skateboarding. In order to learn something about her and her behavior, the company that owns that site's servers would automatically detect that she posted a video file by logging in the type of file that she uploaded (by recognizing the file naming protocol, such as .avi or H.264, for example). The social media site would add that to its database of information about her (name, email, "friends'" email addresses, number of "friends," and so on). That information is structured. The content of the movie, however, is completely unstructured, which is to say that the analytical engines built into the software don't know if it's really a skateboarding video or perhaps something else, and what is actually happening in the video. The video is comprised of millions of bits of information: from the color of her shirt to the weather on the day of filming to the names of the others who are in the scene to the brands of sneakers worn by the skateboarders and on and on and on. If the social media company wanted to glean some insights from her and others' skateboard videos so that it could sell that insight to a skateboard company, it would need a human to watch the video and to identify the styles or brands of sneakers that the skateboarders wear, for instance. They would then log that data for that specific video and for every skateboarding video posted to that site, but that is a painfully slow and expensive means of mining that unstructured data, and most companies cannot afford to spend so much on human labor searching, aggregating, and analyzing the billions of moments of video footage—most of it irrelevant—with the hope that they might spot an emerging trend or glean an insight about skateboarders' sneaker-buying behavior. That same social media company might also want to sell insights it has to cat food companies, and so it might want to hire more humans to review the millions of cat videos… but again, the economics simply don't work out.

Even though a social media company may not be able to glean much from a skateboard video, there are other available resources. Most data carries with it often invisible, companion data about itself—metadata. A single photograph taken with a mobile phone and uploaded to a social media site will include not only the image file and the time stamp of when and from where she uploaded it, it will also likely include exif data from the image file (which indicates the kind of camera or smartphone she used, the make of the lens if any, resolution, the camera settings, and so on) and geo-tagged information about where the photograph was taken, if the camera or camera phone has GPS built in, as most now do. If our skateboarder also tags the other people in the image with her, the company knows where they were on that date, and with whom; they can cross-reference that data with all of the other data that they have on her friends to put together a robust picture of several people's information at that moment. To the social media company hosting her information, the data from the video is evolving from unstructured to structured, from chaos to order.

As a 2011 report from IDC states in its title, "Big Data Is Not the Created Content nor Is It Even Its Consumption—It Is the Analysis of All of the Data Surrounding or Swirling Around It."[20] One can feel the effects of big data in IDC's formulation. No longer do they see data alone as the prize—it is the data about the data that has become the source of new value.

This is the reason that many consider Uber, the ride-share company, to be a big data company and not a car service. Uber, through its smartphone app, database management system, and feedback structure, is able to generate enough supplemental data about its clients, its drivers, and their habits and whereabouts that it can sell that data to other companies and entities that are eager to know more about where people are going, what additional services they might need, and when they are moving about. A traffic management group, for instance, can certainly glean critical insights from knowing the exact patterns of car use in real time every day of the year.

In a certain sense, then, the movement from structured to unstructured data is a movement from facts to meaning. Automated data-mining engines can tell us that it was sixty-six degrees out and drizzling when the skateboard video was posted, but that doesn't relay the grit and dedication of the skateboarders themselves. For that, we need a further level of processing.

Optical character recognition, facial recognition, machine learning, natural language processing, computer vision, neural networks... these are all subfields of artificial intelligence (AI) that bring us tantalizingly close to an unprecedented phase change in automated systems. For instance, if our skateboarder's social media host is also using facial recognition software when they access the unstructured data of her uploaded photographs, she is likely training that software to associate particular visual signatures with her and her friends' identities, meaning that that company may be able to identify her every time a photograph with their faces in it gets uploaded, regardless of whether it's tagged or not with their names. The software would effectively "recognize" her and her friends regardless of whether she's wearing a hat or glasses, or has her hair up.

The rise and proliferation of artificial intelligence in its various forms is a direct outcome of the rise of big data. Once companies began to stockpile vast troves of data that they could feed into supercomputers, AI evolved from a niche research field into the future battleground for those companies that had amassed the most data: Google, Microsoft, Apple, Amazon, and Facebook. It's important to recognize that, like Uber, none of these companies is explicitly a "data" company. Their data collection is a by-product of their primary services, and yet for many of them the buying, selling, mining, and interpreting of data is or will be the lifeblood of their business models. Leaving aside the cyborg nightmares of catastrophists, there is no disagreement that the current and next big waves of technological transformation will involve AI platforms. From the convenience of real-time language translation to the dystopia of predictive policing, AI will shape our lives in ways that even AI's algorithms themselves cannot predict. Our mobile phones, our computers, and our appliances are all collectively and spontaneously generating new reserves of resources from which others will extract wealth, whether we are aware of it or not. Taxi drivers drove us from one place to the next; Uber drivers do that, too, but what they really are doing is supplying fungible data about our habits, our routines, our patterns, our likes, and our dislikes, dumping that into giant "mines" that live on servers. With massive data sets fueling increasingly robust forms of machine learning, are we on the verge of these systems phase-changing from nested scripts into penetrating consciousness?

Whether in the microphysics of ant life and bacteria or in the macrophysics of data becoming "big," the things that now surround us are obeying very different laws as they shrink or grow in scale. What we thought was one thing has become another: A shared ride home has become a data set; an afternoon jog etches in vivid outlines the contours of a secret military base; a digital photograph is the same size even when it's not; and a bacterium can potentially exist in two places at once. And, perhaps most remarkably, out of silica...intelligence. Scale surprises. And cause and effect, it seems, have become decoupled.

Chapter 04

Tiny Violence

In 2013 I walked into the galleries of the International Center for Photography in New York City to view their Triennial exhibition, *A Different Kind of Order*. As I wandered into a back gallery I encountered a very large image of what appeared to be a glorious, glowing sunset sky. The colors blended together in a gradient from a coppery orange to a powdery sky blue. Large in format (almost three feet by six feet), the photograph had no apparent subject. It was all ground and no figure. I stood in front of it, suffused in a wash of sublime color and diffuse light. After basking in the glow for several minutes, I took a step closer to read the title: *Untitled (Reaper Drone)* by Trevor Paglen.

As I stepped away from the photograph, puzzled by the gap between the radiant image and the menacing title, I noticed other museum visitors walking up extremely close to

Fig. 18. *Trevor Paglen,* Untitled (Reaper Drone), *2010. Courtesy of the artist and Metro Pictures, New York.*

the image, scanning their eyes across it, and then pointing to one particular spot. I approached the image a second time. It was then that I found the tiny piece of visual evidence— a figure—that illuminated the gap in meaning between the photograph and its title. Lost in the gauzy color fields was an infinitesimally small speck that was clearly something...and the most likely thing it could be was a drone.

Much of Trevor Paglen's photographic work is visually disorienting—by intention. A political geographer by training, Paglen uses forensic strategies and documentary tools to render visible unseen networks of surveillance, covert operations, and other forms of legal, quasi-legal, and illegal government activities. Filling in blank spaces on "official" maps and capturing the glints of light that reflect off of "invisible" sites, his photographs capture the traces of covert state networks, operations, and operators. Based upon meticulous research and the help of drone spotters and activists around the world, Paglen's work is more than journalism, however. His images do not reveal the whole story in the style of high definition detail that we've come to expect from an infinitely image-able world. Instead, his images and his work place draw us into a space of visual uncertainty.

The power of *Untitled (Reaper Drone)* is that it plays at the same time with both perceptual and conceptual scale. In an interview with the American Civil Liberties Union's Jameel Jaffer about the "aesthetics of surveillance," Paglen describes the role that scale plays in the manifestation of a massive, invisible system:

> [**Q.**] The Utah data center depicted in one of the images we've posted here is reportedly used to store communications obtained through upstream surveillance. The immensity of the data center gives you an idea of the scale of the surveillance. Is the staggering scale of the infrastructure needed to support all of this surveillance something you deliberately set out to convey?
>
> [**A.**] There are a couple of ways in which I try to point towards the scale of surveillance. On one hand,

buildings like the Utah Data Center are so massive and hold so much information that their physicality points to the scale of the programs they support. On the other hand, one of the pieces I like a lot is called "Code Names of the Surveillance State," which is a massive scrolling list of over 4,000 code names for various NSA projects. Individually, they're deliberately nonsensical, but in aggregate I think they give a peek into the scale of the surveillance state.[1]

The drone may only be a speck on the horizon, but it is also larger than life. It is a sentinel and an index of a massive, totalizing state of war, where everyone is potentially visible and in the crosshairs of some surveillance somewhere. Bringing vastness and smallness together in the same frame, Paglen interrupts our daydreaming just as a fly in the soup, a speck in the eye, a stone in the shoe, or a wrench in the works does. In each expression, something tiny has an outsize impact disproportionate to its size. The drone's minuteness in the limitless sky is in inverse proportion to its invisible omnipotence. This is the condition of the constantly surveilled. For those in Afghanistan, Pakistan, and Yemen, and similar at-risk zones, the anxious need to peer over one's shoulder and up into the heavens is a daily occurrence that infiltrates the body and the mind.

The omnipotent drone that Paglen's camera barely spots is both nowhere and everywhere. In the skies above us, size no longer correlates with power: The smaller and the less visible the force, the more total the danger. Scale has become upended. Our world of classical mechanics has trained us to expect a predictable, proportional relationship between cause and effect: that a small push will cause a small movement and a big push a bigger one. But those rules of classical mechanics no longer seem to hold. Perhaps we should label this effect *aproportionality*, akin to asymmetry. The insignificant is unimaginably all-powerful and the unseeable is everywhere. Threat is a permanent condition.

Paglen's photograph reminds us that perturbations in scale are recalibrating both our *perception* and our *conception* of force, power, size, and visibility. Size may no longer matter... but scale still does. And when those disproportionate relationships take form in the realms of combat and surveillance, more is at stake for each of us than feelings of paralysis or frustration. We, and the governmental and nongovernmental bodies that represent us, are collectively remaking warfare and violence through scalar asymmetries. Combine the immaterial capacity to multiply data near infinitely with the entangled networks that shuttle information almost instantaneously around the planet and new relations of scale and power result. These changes are having real effects on real bodies, and because we cannot always perceive them, we risk remaining oblivious to the onslaught. We will look closely at three instances where changes in scale have shifted the terms of combat and recalibrated how violence takes form: in persistent and continuous surveillance that allows us to go backward and forward in time; in the drift toward forms of "netwar" that are no longer state-based but are storming all around us all the time; and in the use and abuse of bits of data to create algorithmic forms of policing that are predictive rather than reactive.

———

The "total warfare" that the almost invisible drones in Trevor Paglen's photographs conjure is equally well illustrated by an emerging technology that promises not only to give us comprehensive visual surveillance, but also the uncanny ability to move backward and forward in time.[2] During the darkest days of the U.S. invasion of Iraq under President George W. Bush, improvised explosive devices (IEDs) were sowing demoralizing chaos for the U.S. operations on the ground. Ross McNutt, formerly an engineer in the U.S. Air Force and then (2004) an instructor at the U.S. Air Force Institute of Technology, challenged his students to help with the war effort. In a project code-named "Project Angel Fire," McNutt and his students, together with military developers, created a "wide field of view persistent surveillance (WFVPS) aerial collection asset," consisting of high-resolution cameras mounted to the undercarriages of military aircraft.[3] The objective was to fly the aircraft continuously in six-hour shifts while taking high-resolution pictures once per second of the entirety of Falluja, Iraq. They then beamed the images down to a control center where they were stitched together into a near-real-time recording of the entire cityscape and archived for future intelligence gathering. If an IED had exploded, analysts could rewind the recordings of the image to the precise time of the detonation. But because they had every second captured and at their fingertips from both before and after the IED's explosion, they could effectively rewind back in time to see whether a truck or group of people had been doing something suspicious at that same location, and then they could also move forward in time from that suspicious act to learn where the potential perpetrators had gone to once they left the scene. And, in theory, they could follow that suspect forward in time to the present moment, even. This would then provide highly reliable intelligence for ground troops or other tactical units to seek out the perpetrators—assuming that the visual evidence was more than circumstantial.

Persistent Surveillance Systems (PSS), the company that McNutt went on to launch, exists because of the intersection of three critical technological vectors: high-resolution digital cameras, low-cost and high-capacity information storage, and high-speed computer processors. In some ways, the basic technology for this kind of surveillance has been available for years: Closed-circuit television cameras have populated our cities and critical infrastructure for decades, as have aerial reconnaissance airplanes. But as with so many similar phenomena, a small shift in scale can precipitously catalyze staggering new capabilities. Increases in speed, resolution, and capacity sparked the possibility that military personnel could surveil every square foot of a twenty-five-square-mile swath of a city (say, Falluja) continuously over the course of the plane's six-hour flight. What makes PSS's technology almost supernatural is the ability of the analyst to move backward and forward in time while zoomed into any point in the image. In other words, near-total visual omniscience. The information is not absolutely continuous (images are recorded at one frame per second rather than thirty, which would provide the illusion of continuous action), but the technology nonetheless approaches a threshold where the map is equal to the territory, or the recording equal to reality.

In the city of Juarez, Mexico, which has been overwhelmed by an astonishingly high rate of murders (three hundred per month) and kidnappings (fifty-two per week), authorities utilized McNutt's system to help gain some control over the violence. By using the equivalent of visual time travel, the police were able to arrest gang members who had ambushed and murdered a female police officer during the daytime in her car. They followed the perpetrators' car and those of several accomplices forward to their ultimate destination and apprehended the suspects there (while also dismantling an entire drug cartel as a result). McNutt contends that the deployment of his technology could reduce crime 30 to 40 percent, resulting in lives and money saved.[4] Abetted by massive data transfer rates and almost unlimited storage capacity, PSS has not just intensified the quantity of surveillance. They have made a qualitative leap into time travel and near-perfect omniscience.

So why are we in the United States not stealing glances over our shoulders already? As you might expect, not everybody is sold on the value of persistent surveillance for domestic settings. While it is still not absolutely total in scope (it cannot see inside of buildings, nor is it as effective at night... though they have developed a night-vision equivalent), citizens are not yet ready to have the system hovering over every public moment of their lives. McNutt and his team, to their credit, understand the stark implications of their system, and they have incorporated advice from the ACLU into its parameters: They do not resolve the imagery to the point where faces are identifiable, nor do they keep the imagery for more than a fixed amount of time (though it's not certain whether the U.S. military is quite as respectful of rights to privacy in other countries). Nonetheless, technologies like these seem often to have a life of their own, insinuating their way into our lives before we even know it. As Paglen's photographs attest, the relative visibility or invisibility of these surveillance technologies is not the point. They are here, and they know all, and their power of time travel would make even H.G. Wells jealous.

———

Since the rise of the information era, changes in technology have rewritten the rules of combat. While state-to-state conflict over physical territory persists, increasingly asymmetrical conflict is the norm, and the terms of combat are being remade almost daily. With these changes, the scale of operations has also changed, to the point where lone individuals operating on the margins of society can wreak havoc in ways that were unimaginable even a decade or two ago. Cyberspying, cyberterror, and cyberwarfare are now as much a part of the terms of war making as guns, bombs, tanks, and armies, leading to situations where asymmetries proliferate and strategists are reinventing the rules of conflict daily.

What is remaking the cultural physics of cause and effect? The near weightless flow of information amplified across total global networks has created the equivalent of a parallel universe with its own physical laws and scalar effects. Those who find ways to master these new rules will predominate. Given that the U.S. Defense Advanced Research Projects Agency (DARPA) built the infrastructure for the internet as we now know it, we would expect their fingerprints to be everywhere across the internet. But ubiquity and scale, in this instance, does not guarantee supremacy, as we shall see. The physics of information flow has its own rules. Google, too, has been instrumental in facilitating the flow of information globally. What is more surprising, however, is that a company that started off building a search engine would, as it has increased in scope and scale, transmogrify into a political player in global counterinsurgencies.

Information networks operate according to properties that make new kinds of behaviors possible in unanticipated ways. Information weighs next to nothing; it is almost infinitely reproducible at little cost; it can be sent to anyplace in the world almost instantaneously; points of access to the network are proliferating precipitously; and it can bear few traces of its creators. In other words, information scales massively through networks. The basic capacity to copy and paste lines of code—a rudimentary function baked into command line text editors from the very beginning—combined with the ability to write simple, executable operations that automate that copying function, has led in a fundamental way to both the explosive growth of the internet and to its core vulnerability. The ease with which humans or machines can duplicate perfectly a line of code or a file or a program and then distribute it—often thousands of times per second—has reconfigured the scale of this digital infrastructure's impact.

A distributed denial of service attack (DDoS) is a lesson in the simple scalability of computer code. A DDoS attack is a highly popular, easily obtainable, low-cost way of crippling web services. It affords a lone operator the possibility of multiplying his intentions by orders of magnitude, driven in part by the easy reproducibility of computer code. DDoS attacks are also now simply a fact of life on the internet. They occur at an alarmingly fast rate and their use continues to increase, despite their relative simplicity. A DDoS attack can shut down the website of an individual, an organization, or a company for anything from seconds to days or weeks.

A DDoS attack, at its most basic, overwhelms the targeted web server with so many requests for information at such a relentlessly high volume that the server cannot perform its basic duty of keeping a website up and running. It is war by scale. The result is a crash of the site's system to anybody who is legitimately trying to access it while the DDoS attack is ongoing. By cybercrime standards a DDoS attack is not very sophisticated, but it remains a successful exploit. What does it cost? A basic one-day service sells from $30 to $70 and a one-week DDoS service sells for $150. A botnet, which is a subterranean means of harnessing enough "zombie" computers to launch an effective attack, costs $700, though most botnets are not sold in marketplaces but are instead handcrafted by the hackers themselves.[5]

Thus, for less than $1,000, an individual operating out of a basement can enlist a silent, nearly invisible army of thousands to launch a weeklong attack that can cripple and shut down the most public-facing component of a billion-dollar, multinational corporation so that hundreds of thousands, if not millions, of users and customers are affected. And this happens over and over and over again. Imagine that same individual, before the internet: What would he have at his disposal to cause such turmoil? Clearly, the terms of engagement have changed, and the scale of the asymmetry is tilted even further.

In 2013 Google launched their Digital Attack Map, a visual dashboard that tracks, aggregates, and represents visually the flow of DDoS attacks in real time.[6] According to Google's site, the security firm Arbor Networks estimates the number of DDoS attacks at greater than two thousand per day. Trying to give form to an otherwise invisible, distributed army of attackers, the Digital Attack Map uses arcs of colored, dotted lines that skitter across a map of the world to represent the source and the target (whether internal to countries or across borders), the type, and the volume of attacks. A histogram along the bottom of the screen displays the data across time, giving a longitudinal scan of the peaks and valleys of attacks from the present back over two years. It's possible, even, to "play" the histogram like a movie, watching the attacks surge and recede across the map over time like a fireworks show running forward and backward in time. Remarkably, given the spectacular nature of the show, the visualization represents only the top 2 percent of DDoS attacks. Each day of the timeline is also accompanied by news headlines that document the unrelenting attacks.

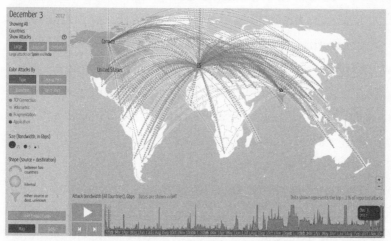

Fig. 19. *Sources and targets of distributed denial of service attacks on the Digital Attack Map (a collaboration of Google Ideas and Arbor Networks).*

Cybersecurity firm Imperva Incapsula released an analysis of its data, titled "Q2 2015 Global DDoS Threat Landscape: Assaults Resemble Advanced Persistent Threats."[7] Their data indicates a continuous upward trend of the size of DDoS attacks, peaking at 253 gigabytes per second in the second quarter of 2015. Their key findings:

> On one hand we observed long, complex, multiphase assaults that resemble advanced persistent threats (APT). These employ different methods and can last days, weeks, and even months at [a] time. On the other hand, we also noted a preponderance of rudimentary single-vector attacks usually lasting no longer than 30 minutes.
>
> To us, this duality relates to two main DDoS offender archetypes, the first being the professional cybercriminal, the second being a user of botnet-for-hire services—so called "booters" (or "stressers"). Their subscription-based model offers anybody the ability to launch several short-lived DDoS attacks for just a few dozen dollars a month.

Incapsula pays its bills by scaring the daylights out of potentially vulnerable companies, so they are predisposed to hyping the data, but they do paint a vivid scene. What stands out, however, is the sheer accessibility of this tactic and the ease with which Davids can stun and cripple Goliaths.

DDoS attacks are only one form of digital malfeasance. Unlike other, more permanently damaging tactics such as publishing or selling stolen data and ransomware (freezing a victim's computer until a ransom is paid to unlock it), DDoS attacks gum up everyday operating for a business but rarely do lasting damage. The forms of cyberattack are myriad, and a testament both to the ingenuity of the attackers and the plasticity of the form. Thousands happen each and every day, and the malware amplified by network effects allow lone operators to have an outsized impact upon the digital landscape, though the actors in these attacks often fit very different profiles from the hardened, rogue operators of past conflicts.

To get a better sense of the complexion of cybercrime and some of the criminals who help to perpetrate it, a quick scan of the headlines of major news outlets reveals the contours of this new landscape:

- "15-Year-Old Arrested for Hacking 259 Companies" (ZDNet)[8]
- "Teen Held over Cyber Attacks Targeting US Government" (NBCnews.com)[9]
- "Teenager in Northern Ireland Is Arrested in TalkTalk Hacking Case" (*New York Times*)[10]
- "The Boy Hackers: Teenagers Accessed the CIA, USAF, NHS, Sony, Nintendo...and the Sun" (the *Sun*)[11]
- "Six Bailed Teenagers Accused of Cyber Attacks Using Lizard Squad Tool" (the *Guardian*)[12]

- "Teen Who Hacked CIA Director's Email Tells How He Did It" (*Wired*)[13]

We have certainly entered a new era of scalar asymmetry when teenagers are able to break into the supposedly secure email account of the director of the U.S. Central Intelligence Agency. And the headlines, just a few sampled from an internet search, reinforce the picture that the modality of threat to security is no longer simply state to state, as it has been for centuries, but now includes lone teenage boys (mostly boys) operating from their basements using ordinary, off-the-shelf hardware. While many of these incidents are pranks gone bad, the twenty-first-century equivalent of joyriding in a "borrowed" car in the suburbs, there is something qualitatively different about them. In part this is because the impact of their actions is indistinguishable from the thousands of similar attacks that take place every day. They are part of a swarming mass of indistinguishable assaults that pulse across networks while we work, watch, and fritter away hours online. We remain blissfully unaware of the buzzing criminal activity because most of it is silent, invisible, and undetectable to our senses. Starting the ignition of a car and driving off in it leaves a trace; fingerprints on an abandoned car are a trace; launching an executable file from an anonymized proxy server on an unsuspecting computer user's hard drive makes no such disturbance.

The scalar asymmetry of these operations, from the small-time hack to state-sponsored spying, and their relative quiet, leaves us in a new condition of almost imperceptible but permanent cyberwarfare. The Digital Attack Map is but one way to understand the scope of the activity. The cross-border attacks—from China to the United States, from the U.S. to China, from Iran to the U.S., from Syria to Israel, from Argentina to Australia, from Luxembourg to Peru, from Turkey to Hong Kong (and with the entire continent of Africa having the unfortunate distinction of almost complete quietude... an indicator of their strategic and cyber-isolation)—paint an indelible picture of a third world war that seems to be raging all around us all of the time but that few, except perhaps the victims and perpetrators, are aware of.

The scope of these incidences, however, is setting off alarms. A 2015 *New York Times* article suggests, "Over the last four years, foreign hackers have stolen source code and blueprints to the oil and water pipelines and power grid of the United States and have infiltrated the Department of Energy's networks 150 times... The number of attacks against industrial control systems more than doubled to 675,186 in January 2014 from 163,228 in January 2013, according to Dell Security—most of those in the United States, Britain and Finland."[14] It is worth pausing and reflecting upon the numbers: 675,186 attacks. In one month. The numbers are so large (and the increase is actually more than fourfold) that it raises profound ontological questions about this activity: Is it war by other means? Is it peace? Business as usual? The new normal? It is certainly a qualitatively new condition brought about by the shift in scale that networked information systems enable. Spying has existed for centuries, but this represents something other than that. It is also happening on a playing field that does not look like the traditional battlefield, where powerful nations with powerful militaries confronted one another. As Michael V. Hayden, former head of the U.S. National Security Agency, suggests, "Despite all the talks of a cyber–Pearl Harbor, I am not really worried about a state competitor like China doing catastrophic damage to infrastructure…It's the attack from renegade, lower-tier nation-states that have nothing to lose."[15] Hayden neglects to point out that in many of these incidences, the culprits are not nation-state players but are instead rhizomatic groups of operators with little to no state affiliation. They range in character and intent from script kiddies and hactivists to paramilitary organizations and organized crime. In a 2001 Rand Corporation report titled *The Future of Terror, Crime, and Militancy*, John Arquilla and David Ronfeldt coined the term *netwar* to describe this new, asymmetrical, distributed, non-state configuration:

> The term netwar refers to an emerging mode of conflict (and crime) at societal levels, short of traditional military warfare, in which the protagonists use

network forms of organization and related doctrines, strategies, and technologies attuned to the information age. These protagonists are likely to consist of dispersed organizations, small groups, and individuals who communicate, coordinate, and conduct their campaigns in an internetted manner, often without a precise central command...

The netwar spectrum also includes a new generation of revolutionaries, radicals, and activists who are beginning to create information-age ideologies, in which identities and loyalties may shift from the nation state to the transnational level of "global civil society." New kinds of actors, such as anarchistic and nihilistic leagues of computer-hacking "cyboteurs," may also engage in netwar.

Many—if not most—netwar actors will be non-state, even stateless. Some may be agents of a state, but others may try to turn states into *their* agents.[16]

What they capture in this sketch is, in effect, the emergence of a new kind of organizational counterlogic that is fluid, dispersed, and highly reconfigurable—like a stable solid that has phase-changed into a viscous liquid. The familiarity, for better or worse, of traditional nation-state conflict has mutated into a leaderless form of quicksilver that evades our grasp and can reconfigure itself into endless combinatorial forms.

It's not surprising that we are bedazzled by the power of data to inflict real harm. But, as we saw in chapter 2, the quantification of experience into data embodies its own forms of violence. Inviting us to linger in that gap between data and experience, the artists Keith and Mendi Obadike draw us in with the quiet allure of numbers, and they then shatter the cool contours of the quantitative. *Numbers Station [Furtive Movements]*, their live performance work that debuted in 2015 at the Ryan Lee Gallery in New York City, alerts us to the messy transformations in kind that happen when lived events become reduced to numbers.[17] The performance consists of the couple sitting on opposite sides of two adjoined tables. Each is wearing headphones and speaking into microphones as they alternate reciting short strings of numbers over a twenty-five-minute span that they also simultaneously broadcast both in the gallery and on shortwave radio, "048, 276, 049, 394, 050, 366, 052, 308, 060, 425, 061, 203, 062, 100, 063, 357…"[18]

Their breathy, monotonous, almost mechanical back-and-forth recitation of these numbers (accompanied by eerie, tonal background music) mimics the form of numbers stations. Numbers stations, for the uninitiated, are regular shortwave radio broadcasts that date back to World War I. Enigmatic and obscure, they feature the narration of lists of numbers thought to be encrypted communication from governments to their covert operatives in the field. There is a

Fig. 20. *Mendi and Keith Obadike,* Numbers Station [Furtive Movements]. *Photo by Imani Romney-Rosa. Courtesy of Obadike Studio.*

lively subculture of shortwave radio enthusiasts who track and record these mysterious broadcasts. In contrast, however, the Obadikes are reading anonymous case numbers from police logs of incidences of those who were caught in the nets of New York City's controversial stop-and-frisk policing strategy. This approach to policing (which ran from 2002 to 2016 until it was struck down in a ruling by Judge Shira Scheindlin) targeted "furtive movements" with the aim to preempt more serious criminal behavior before it happened. In reality, though, its impact on reducing crime during those years was minimal at best; its impact on the communities it targeted is inestimable. The American Civil Liberties Union of New York analyzed the data and found that of the 685,724 stops that took place in 2011: 53 percent were of African-Americans, 34 percent were of Hispanics, 51 percent were of people between the ages of fourteen and twenty-one, and 88 percent of those stopped were not arrested. During its fifteen-year run, more than five million innocent New Yorkers were stopped and frisked, and the vast majority of those were young persons of color.

It is the lives shattered by systemic racism and violence that haunts the Obadikes' hypnotic installation. Their flat, artificial delivery style draws our attention to the obscene reductiveness of the data. People reduced to three-digit case numbers. Five million lives altered by a policy that many ignored, if our skin color allowed. We like to think that data is innocent, that it is simply tiny facts that live somewhere in the ether, like water, coal, or uranium. But in the phase change from experience to information, we tend to overlook the violence that precipitates that transformation. The Obadikes reverse engineer the statistics, breathing the texture of lives shattered back into each tiny bit of data.

Chapter 05

The Numb of Numbers

It turns out that a billion is not a billion everywhere. And, as recently as the 1970s, countries as deeply connected in history, tradition, and trade as the United States and Great Britain had a fundamentally different way to calculate what comprised a billion.[1] Perhaps it is a testament to the sheer scale of a billion that we seem to have avoided major international conflict despite having dramatically different ideas about how large this number actually is. One could argue that it is so large that we've rarely had use for it, except in mathematics. Until recently, in fact, billions described most everything we could conceivably encounter or count in the physical world, until our economies started to balloon up in size to the point where a trillion became necessary in common parlance.

Up until 1974, those in Great Britain followed the long scale system, meaning that one billion was equal to one million millions. This will immediately strike any U.S. reader as incorrect, and quite shockingly so.[2] The United States, which follows the short scale model, considers one billion to be one thousand millions, and one trillion to be one thousand billions, and so on. A short scale billion is thus a thousand times smaller than a long scale billion. And a short scale trillion is a million times smaller than a long scale trillion (which is equal to the short scale quintillion). If we zoom out beyond the two countries we see that things get even more complicated, both in terms of the numbering systems used and the linguistic translations. Australia, Brazil, Hong Kong, Kenya, and the United States all use the short scale; Argentina, Germany, Iran, Venezuela, and Senegal use the long scale. And some countries (Canada, South Africa, and Puerto Rico) even use both.[3] The Indian number system divides numbers differently, separating numerals with commas after three digits, and then every two subsequent digits. For example, the Arabic 100,000 is written 1,00,000 in the Indian (or Vedic) system. Similarly, the number 123,456,789 (Arabic) is written 12,34,56,789 in the Vedic system. A different, more linguistically oriented way to compare the two systems reveals that in the Vedic system the significant groupings of numbers are not a thousand, a million, and a billion, but are instead one hundred thousand (*lakh*) and ten million (*crore*).[4] We also see this global variation in China and other countries. Those in China, for instance, use up to three different numbering systems, depending on the context of use.

		SHORT SCALE	LONG SCALE
10^0	1	one	one
10^1	10	ten	ten
10^2	100	hundred	hundred
10^3	1000	thousand	thousand
10^6	1,000,000	million	million
10^9	1,000,000,000	billion	thousand million
10^{12}	1,000,000,000,000	trillion	billion
10^{15}	1,000,000,000,000,000	quadrillion	thousand billion
10^{18}	1,000,000,000,000,000,000	quintillion	trillion

Fig. 21. *Diagram comparing short and long scales.*

A recent *BBC News Magazine* article asked, "Is Trillion the New Billion?" That there is still a need to clarify what a trillion is—thereby avoiding a simple semantic error that results in a thousandfold miscalculation—in a major British newspaper in 2011 is a testament to the pervasiveness of the misunderstanding. The error is so common that the *BBC News Magazine* included in a sidebar a short primer attempting to explain to its UK readers what, precisely, a billion and trillion are today.[5] While the concept of a trillion is seeping more frequently into our daily vocabulary, it was not always the case. For the generations that lived through most of the twentieth century, a *trillion* was a rare encounter. The equivalent today is the term *quadrillion*. Ask yourself: When was the last time that you used the word *quadrillion*? Possibly never.

Quantities like a billion or a trillion can be challenging to comprehend, despite the fact that most teenagers are able to grasp the mathematical concept (as they are usually obliged to in math class when they learn scientific notation). Just as the metrological development of "physical constants" progressively decoupled measurement from things we could hold or touch, numbers in the billions and the trillions also tend to elude human perception and experience. One can count to a million in about twelve days, to a billion would take about thirty-two years, but to count to a trillion would take over thirty-one thousand years—about as long as human civilization has existed. Which is to say that a person could not do it. These gigantic numbers matter and yet, somehow, they don't quite matter.[6] Their remove from our everyday perceptions means that they live, for most of us, in the realm of fantasy, in the range of "zillions and gazillions."[7] We are at the mercy of metaphors, analogies, and flights of imagination to give true scope and scale to the numbers that are more and more frequently part of our everyday lexicon.

There is an oft-quoted passage that is variously attributed to Joseph Stalin (though it has never been confirmed), "The death of one man is a tragedy; the death of millions is a statistic." How is it that we can be so moved to respond to the suffering of one individual and yet so callous when confronted with the death of hundreds of thousands or millions? Why does the outrage and compassion not scale linearly? When the numbers ramp up, why does the affective charge decline? There is a numbing quality to numbers of great size.[8] We are drawn emotionally to stories and images that convey the suffering of one individual, and yet we seem to shut down when that number gets much larger than two or three. The absence of the possibility of representing the mass loss of human life in some ways alters our ability to process it. We must be reminded to "never forget" holocausts of various populations, as if our emotional faculties reject grappling with these massive losses of human life.

How can we put into perspective in our everyday lives the waves of abstract, immaterial information that currently washes over us: military budgets in the trillions of dollars, 340 mass shootings in the United States in 2018, or more than $6.5 billion spent on the presidential and congressional campaigns in 2016.[9] The key is to develop strategies that reconnect our bodies and our senses to these abstracted experiences in ways that help us to live more highly attuned to the very small and the very large...and yet not get paralyzed by them in the process. Using very different means, the following four projects, each a creative response to a contemporary tendency to become numb to the scale of the world today, attempt to reconnect us to sensory cues as a means for linking our capacity to comprehend to the vast scale of problems we have unleashed. They use techniques such as *translation* and *materialization* to bring human, sensory presence back into the space of the unthinkable. And while they originate in the realm of the arts for the most part, that doesn't mean they bear no relation to our everyday context. We can draw lessons from these more spectacular and extreme strategies to envision new ways to make unthinkable situations more possible.

In his site titled Information Is Beautiful, for instance, designer David McCandless utilizes the techniques of information design to wrestle with a variety of contemporary political, social, and scientific issues.[10] Flummoxed by the scale of numbers that are tossed around in the media, McCandless produced in 2009 (and since updated in 2013) a wondrous

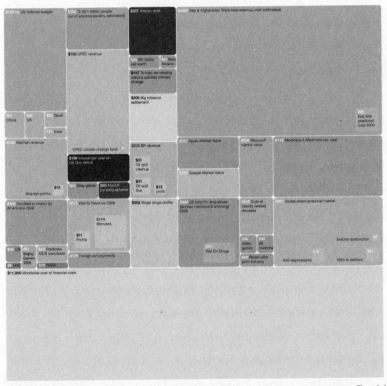

Fig. 22. *David McCandless, Billion Dollar-o-Gram, courtesy David McCandless@informationisbeautiful.net.*

visualization he terms "The Billion Dollar-o-Gram." A patchwork of cheerily colored rectangles, this simple diagram juxtaposes quantities of billions of dollars, helping us to see the relative costs of diverse social programs and projects.

The designer's canniness emerges in the subtle contiguities of neighboring tiles in the diagram (the amounts below are in the billions of dollars):

- the cost of eradicating AIDS ($64) worldwide sidles up next to *Wall Street Revenue in 2009* ($371)
- *OPEC revenue* ($780) dwarfs the estimated cost ($300) *To Lift 1 Billion People out of Poverty*
- the *Global Pharmaceutical Market* ($825) outstrips *U.S. Medicare and Medicaid costs* combined ($742)
- and the *World Wide Porn Industry* ($40) outpaces by a large margin the markets for *Antidepressants* ($19) plus *Erectile Dysfunction* ($6) combined

The diagram is dominated, however, by one massive rectangle that seems to loom over the vast agglomeration of markets and costs—the *Worldwide Cost of the Financial Crisis* ($11,900). We may not fully, phenomenologically grasp what $11,900 (billion) amounts to, but we can easily visually weigh how preposterously massive that is compared to the $147 (billion) spent *To help developing nations combat climate change*. The sad ironies of our global priorities become crystal clear. By juxtaposing like with like and compiling those into a single frame, McCandless's tiles translate the vast back to a human scale and put the numbers into reach, so to speak. What makes McCandless's strategy uniquely effective is the way in which that translation takes form. By creating categories such as *fighting*, *giving*, *hustling*, and *losing* he humanizes the numbers, putting them into frames that mimic our own ways of spending and accumulating. They bring these abstractions home to our own actions. How can this relate to more quotidian situations?

A home purchase experience often ends up with the buyers suddenly throwing around huge numbers as if they were missing several zeros. The scale of the purchase is so outsize that one starts to think, "Well, what's the difference between $85K and $95K in the big scheme of things?" It begins to feel like the difference between $85 and $95. But translate that ten-thousand-dollar difference into alternative, meaningful units (classes at the community college, student loan forgiveness, international trips, visits to see friends, or weeks of groceries) and then the numbers actually mean something that is graspable in terms of everyday experience. One can then decide whether the fancier new house is really worth missing out on four semesters at the community college or five trips to the tropics in the dead of winter. As numbers climb in scale, it's almost as if they phase-change from the real or material to the abstract, and our task is to wrench them back into units that make a difference to our everyday experience. We can see the process of translation take stunning form as well in Chris Jordan's work *Running the Numbers*, in which he reconfigures the imponderability of global climate change into something we can all grasp, literally—a plastic beverage bottle.

Fig. 23. *"Plastic Bottles, 2007," from the series* Running the Numbers: An American Self-Portrait (2006–current), *by Chris Jordan. Depicts two million plastic beverage bottles, the number used in the U.S. every five minutes [2007].*

Fig. 24. *Chris Jordan, "Plastic Bottles, 2007"—detail.*

If the death of a million is a statistic, is there a way for us to more fully grasp the lineage and lasting impact on our American experience of four hundred years of slavery and inequality?[11] At thirty-five feet tall and seventy-five feet long, Kara Walker's redolent female sphinx squats majestically in the dim light of an abandoned sugar factory. Molasses still drips from the walls while oversized candy babies (molded from liquid sugar) stand alongside this regal and raunchy sphinx-woman. Seemingly built entirely of refined sugar, the mammoth figure inhabited the decaying, stale-smelling Domino Sugar factory on the banks of the East River in Brooklyn, New York, in 2014. Colossal in scale, Walker's full title for the piece was as long as the installation was ambitious: *A Subtlety, or the Marvelous Sugar Baby, an Homage to the unpaid and overworked Artisans who have refined our Sweet tastes from the cane fields to the Kitchens of the New World on the Occasion of the demolition of the Domino Sugar Refining Plant.* Its uncanny effects came from mixing sensorial immersion and conceptual paradoxes together in equal degrees.

Glowing, as if emerging from a pile of white sugar, her sweet colossus flaunts our cultural ideals of monumentality. Sweet and bitter, brown (molasses) and white (sugar), racial stereotype and regal statue, subtle and showy, carnal and maternal, domesticated and transcendent, a miniature made massive—the piece refuses to settle into a singular narrative. Walker seized upon a premodern sugar confection (a "subtlety" was a molded sugar sculpture that was common to the meals of medieval nobles) and inflated it to massive scale. Sugar, of course, is a sweet with a bitter secret, as it is an industry that was built upon the broken backs of slaves in the West Indies. And it is what poisons us now—cheap and plentiful today—leading to epidemics of obesity, which themselves disproportionately target poor communities of color. By transforming a tiny, banal confection into a prodigious reflection upon race, racism, and empire building, Walker provokes us to revisit the horrors upon which the wonder of our empire was built. Our physical disorientation at the scale of the "marvelous sugar baby" comes in relation to the millions of lives

Fig. 25. *Kara Walker,* A Subtlety, or the Marvelous Sugar Baby, an Homage to the unpaid and overworked Artisans who have refined our Sweet tastes from the cane fields to the Kitchens of the New World on the Occasion of the demolition of the Domino Sugar Refining Plant, *2014, Polystyrene foam, sugar, Approx. 35.5 x 26 x 75.5 feet (10.8 x 7.9 x 23 m), Installation view: Domino Sugar Refinery, A project of Creative Time, Brooklyn, NY, 2014, Photo: Jason Wyche. © Kara Walker, courtesy of Sikkema Jenkins & Co., New York.*

erased in the slave trade that fueled the journey from brown sugar cane to the white sugar on our tabletops. A bitter tang of blood mixes with the sweetness...as repulsion does with awe. Four hundred years of inequality is a statistic; through its scale and sensory presence, the *Marvelous Sugar Baby* makes that story felt again in our own time.

By spinning tragedy into sugar, Walker takes an historical, statistical fact and makes it present to our senses. Her process of materialization counteracts the drift toward heady abstraction and immateriality. She does this through the site-specific smells, the dim light of the cavernous warehouse, and the physical mass of the sculpted subtlety. We are dwarfed by its massiveness and humbled by our puniness.

If measurement and immateriality trace the gradual drifting away of understanding from human, corporeal perception, Walker's work points us toward another path forward: We must make statistics and abstractions part of our lived, material experiences. In surprising ways, we manage to "disappear" global problems through the systems we set up and the habits we inculcate. We don't perceive the rise in temperatures in the summer because heated and air-conditioned buildings make the climate nearly invisible to our senses. But if we progressively let the temperatures of our buildings drift upward in the summer in parallel with global warming we may be reminded in subtle, sensory ways that our actions are having collective impact on our climate. This is a strategy that the Japanese government actually proposed in 2005, turning air conditioners' thermostats from seventy-seven to eighty-two degrees in the summer and encouraging men to abandon the traditional suit and tie in favor of short-sleeved shirts. Today, Japanese government buildings dim their lights for an hour in the middle of the day as a reminder of the need to combat global environmental change.[12] The aim of this strategy is to give its workers sensory cues that index and look to combat the nearly invisible drift toward a cataclysmic future.

If we want to help our elective representatives to understand the inverse relationship of Defense Department budget increases to federal disinvestment in education, perhaps we should invite these politicians to work for a day during a heat wave in the suffocating swelter of an underfunded public school. These schools' lack of air-conditioning—and the direct impact that this has on the capacity of their students to learn and be productive—might suddenly make the obscenity of increases to a trillion-dollar U.S. defense budget that much more palpable. Or touring a server farm or an Amazon retail distribution center might help us to recognize that the "weightless" and "frictionless" economy of the internet cannot survive without massive commitments of industrial-age raw materials.

Even the unplanned disruptions of garbage strikes can help us to put our hyperconsumption into perspective. When these strikes reveal the hideous buildup of our waste streams and force us to confront what it might mean to live with our disposables for more than a few days, we must reconsider the cost of "disappearing" our trash and disposing of it in areas that are out of sight and mind. Keeping hold of those for a month or two would be an even more potent sensory reminder to minimize our production of waste.

Each of these strategies makes the abstractions of scale palpable—even though some of them may do so in uncomfortable ways. But why shouldn't we be uncomfortable with climate change, with systemic inequality, or broken systems? Maybe we need to feel them more than we need to intellectualize them. How can we find ways to counteract the drift toward abstraction and the dematerialization of lived experience into ones and zeroes? Hendrik Hertzberg published a book of one million dots (five thousand dots per page for two hundred pages). Why? He wanted to help us to experience "one million of—*something*."[13] Materializing one million of

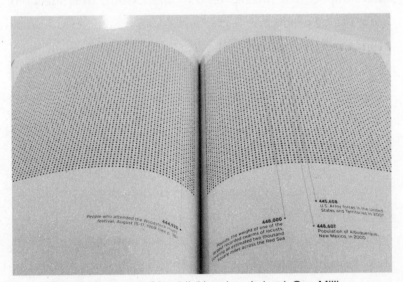

Fig. 26. *Page from Hendrik Hertzberg's book* One Million.

something and putting it into the palms of our hands can help us try to grasp the weighty urgency of scale.

The scale of the things that have a real impact on our lived experience—military budgets, pollutants in the air, collective student debt, lives lost in genocides, murders in our cities, the rise in global temperatures, the salaries of CEOs—often seem beyond our capacity to grasp them. Their collective evaporation leaves us facing a fog that we can barely see through. Disoriented—fumbling forward toward concepts that slip through our fingers—we are both drawn into the mist in search of some deeper truth while filled with dread that we will not grasp anything solid. We need strategies—translation and materialization are two—that bring these numbers out of quantitative abstraction and back into our human sensorium. Stories and images can be the bridges back from the mystification of the vast and the unthinkably large.

Chapter 06

Scalar Framing

The photograph is officially known as AS17-148-22727, a humdrum name for a revolutionary image. The crew of the Apollo 17 mission took the iconic image on December 7, 1972,[1] and ever since it has seared itself into the public's visual imagination. Colloquially known as the "Blue Marble," the photograph is striking in its clarity and simplicity: planet Earth—the oblate spheroid planet reduced to a flat, near perfect, circle—isolated against a black ground, or void. Ruddy continents peek out from underneath frothy swirls of white clouds while the Antarctic polar ice cap peeks out from the globe's underside. Almost immediately upon publication, environmental movements adopted and circulated the image on posters and in communications, undoubtedly moved by the photograph's sublime combination of beauty and vulnerability.

In visual terms, what had once been the ultimate in

pictorial ground—the surface of Earth—had, in the click of a shutter, flipped to become a fathomable figure (now set against the cosmos). While we had understood for centuries that we lived on a round planet, here we were looking back at ourselves, and our very real physical limits, from a startling, omniscient vantage. Through the photograph, our world— our everything—was made knowable and visually consumable. Ground had become figure, and the infinite had become

Fig. 27. *NASA, AS17-148-22727, 1972 (aka the "Blue Marble").*

finite. By shrinking our whole world into the palms of our hands, so to speak, we did not make ourselves godlike in our omniscience, but more bounded in our global fortunes.

This extrapolation and transformation of our visual system from earthbound to cosmic turns up in another iconic, visual work from that same era, *Powers of Ten*. Chances are, depending on your age and background, that you encountered this masterwork of twentieth-century design during a science or math class in middle school, whether you recognized it as great design or simply a break from the teacher's usual class plan. Like Disney's *Donald in Mathmagic Land*, Charles and Ray Eames's nine-minute film became a staple of the U.S. public school curriculum in the second half of the twentieth century—a brief, dazzling respite of colorful cinematic digression in an otherwise gray monotony of textbook exercises, quizzes, and unending homework assignments.

Wife and husband team Ray and Charles Eames designed the kind of things that most people think of when they imagine the products of design: chairs, tables, houses, posters, toys, books, and so on. But what distinguishes them, beyond the accessible brilliance of their work, is the originality of their vision. Their eclectic output took off in the 1940s and roared through to the latter part of the 1970s, encompassing not just products but also films, reports, exhibitions, and experiences. More than just accomplished form givers, the Eameses used their diverse talents to catalyze thinking and seeing differently. Their films, of which they produced dozens, are sly object lessons in acute observation, pattern, structure, and everyday beauty.

Blacktop, shot in 1952, is an eleven-minute meditation on nothing more than soapy water flowing across the blacktop in a school play yard. Set to Bach's *Goldberg Variations*, the film's entrancing pace and unremitting focus upon the water compels the viewer to find rhythm, pattern, movement, flow, and, ultimately, inherent beauty in something we would otherwise easily overlook. Their 1957 film *Toccata for Toy Trains*, scored by legendary Hollywood composer Elmer Bernstein, follows the comings and goings of a tiny world comprised of toys and toy trains, creating a fantasy of bustling village life set in an artificial, scaled-down landscape. The camera lens is poised at the level of the train tracks and uses a shallow depth of field, which immerses the viewer into the scene at the scale of the toys themselves. Charles Eames narrates a two-minute introductory meditation on the value of truth to materials, the critical importance of toys, and the inherent differences between scale models and toy trains. Thirteen minutes in total length, the remaining eleven minutes consist of the trains themselves and the fantasy space that they construct, with nothing but Bernstein's buoyant score alongside. Many of their films—acutely observational and focused on ephemera—train our vision, encouraging us to consider the overlooked, the undervalued, and the mysteriously ordinary. *Powers of Ten* (1977), perhaps their most iconic film, takes us on a dazzling visual journey, along the way establishing a groundbreaking framework for thinking through scale.

The movie itself is an almost effortless formal exercise. Its gee-whiz, seamless leaps across space and time easily distract us from the conceptual heavy lifting that goes on below the surface. *Powers of Ten* (subtitled *A Film Dealing with the Relative Size of Things in the Universe...And the Effect of Adding Another Zero*, and originally made for IBM) was itself inspired by a 1957 book titled *Cosmic View: The Universe in 40 Jumps*, by Kees Boeke.[2] A syncopated, blippy soundtrack (also by Elmer Bernstein) introduces a brief title sequence, as Philip Morrison, the film's narrator, then briefs us on the method that will underlie the film's structure. "The picnic near the lakeside in Chicago is the start of a lazy afternoon, early one October. We begin with a scene, one meter wide, which we view from just one meter away. Now every ten seconds we will look from ten times farther away, and our field of view will be ten times wider." The film opens with a view of a couple lounging on a blanket in a field of green grass, but as the narration commences, the camera angle shifts to one situated directly above the couple, in the sky—a bird's-eye or plan view. As the camera appears to accelerate upward in the sky, simple graphics frame and illustrate the shift in scale. A white graphic square, ten meters wide, runs like a boundary around the picnickers on the field of green, fencing in our view and providing our first frame of reference.

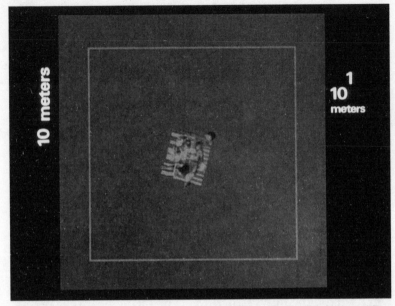

Fig. 28. *Film frame from* Powers of Ten *(1977), a film by Charles and Ray Eames © 1977, 2020 Eames Office, LLC (eamesoffice.com).*

The film cleverly constructs a three-dimensional unit of space, starting at ten meters cubed, that will form the basis of our viewing throughout. At the first power of ten, the subject is self-evident: a couple lounging on a picnic blanket on a sunny day. Initially, the couple on their blanket fills the frame, yet slowly they shrink in relative size as the camera pulls upward into the sky. "Our picture will center on the picnickers, even after they've been lost to sight…one hundred meters wide," Morrison's voice continues, "the distance a man can run in ten seconds." The camera continues to zoom out. "This square is a kilometer wide…We see the great city on the lake shore." The camera continues to magically float upward, as if dragged by an alien spacecraft. It races away from the picnickers, and by the time we're at ten to the seventh power, we reach this remarkable moment: "We are able to see the whole Earth."

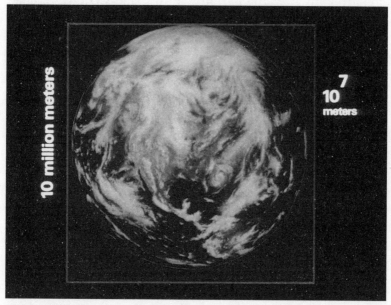

Fig. 29. *Film frame from* Powers of Ten *(1977), a film by Charles and Ray Eames © 1977, 2020 Eames Office, LLC (eamesoffice.com).*

The urgent narration and the zooming camera will reach its apex at 10^{24}, when we become a speck, dwarfed by the vastness of the cosmos.

From there, the camera rapidly zooms back in to the couple, reversing each power of ten in two seconds instead of ten, until momentarily pausing upon the reclining couple still at rest on their picnic blanket. From there, the camera performs its next trick: zooming in by a power of ten to the microscopic level, starting with the man's hand that rests on his belly. It miraculously burrows deeper into the skin, then from there to the cellular, molecular, and even atomic levels, reaching its end at 10^{-16} (or 0.000001 ångstrom). As the film glides from 10^{-14} to 10^{-16} the narrator admits that we have reached the limits of our own knowledge, "As a single proton fills our screen, we reach the edge of present understanding. Are these some quarks at intense interaction?"

Powers of Ten is not just a conceptual marvel, but it is also a work of stunning technical animation. In 1977 the Eameses did not have at their disposal the modern wizardry of computer-generated special effects. It should not be surprising to learn that the Eameses drew upon diverse disciplinary backgrounds to produce a film that so powerfully reframed our understanding of numbers, while also threading a through line from the most distant horizons of our cosmos to the invisibilia that makes up our known world. The Eameses' collaborators on the book and film, Philip and Phylis Morrison, brought their own particular disciplinary talents to the project: Philip Morrison was a professor of physics and astronomy at MIT, and Phylis Morrison taught science and art to children and their teachers.

From two picnickers to the city of Chicago to the whole Earth to quarks and the limits of our knowledge, the Eameses' *Powers of Ten* takes us on a ride that forcefully and continuously reframes our point of view. For those who have never had the opportunity to watch *Powers of Ten*, the effect they developed has nonetheless become embedded in our everyday experience, thanks to the ubiquity of digital navigation applications. Google Maps, founded in 2005, incorporated the same visual construct of a dynamic, zooming camera that frames successively larger or smaller units of land into its Maps application. Our facility with zooming in and out of a spatial map or satellite image has become second nature now, but it found its more powerful articulation in *Powers of Ten*. Masterful in its visual agility, our journey from the couple's relaxing idyll in the Chicago park by the lakeshore to our luminous planet's swift disappearance into the cosmos is, throughout, accompanied by the comforting white frame of the Eameses' invention.

From the couple to the city to the planet to the universe, each successive zoom outward or inward reframes the view, giving us new information, new insights, and a new context for consideration. At 10^1 the interpersonal dynamics of the couple at rest come to the fore; at 10^3 we see Chicago, where the lifestyle of the middle-class, picnicking couple exists in stark contrast to what we don't see, the tensions around race, inequality, and justice that were troubling and still trouble the city; at 10^7 we reflect upon the planet and its environmental precariousness; at 10^{24} more existential questions arise, as we become an immeasurably tiny speck whose insignificance is proportional to our role in the cosmos…and so on back down to the subatomic level as well. With each focal shift in scale the problems, the challenges, the opportunities, and the contexts shift as well. Framing puts content and context in dynamic tension. It obscures concerns while exposing others—revealing and focusing at each successive vantage.

———

What can we learn from the Eameses' *Powers of Ten* that might help us better understand and engage with scale, complexity, and systems change today? I believe we can gently reorient its focus and utilize the sliding scale of each power of ten to slice through the entanglements of problems to illuminate strategies for taming that complexity—or at least engaging more productively with it. To do this, we will use a method that I call *scalar framing*, a fluid, conceptual framework for challenging assumptions, inviting collaboration, and locating points of leverage in the problem space where points of leverage may not be self-evident. The powers-of-ten framework that the Eameses developed can map neatly onto social units, though these function more as analogies than as hard and fast categories: It can be helpful, for instance, to think of 10^1 as the scale of the individual; 10^2 as the family; 10^3 as the neighborhood; 10^4 as the community; 10^5 as the city; 10^6 as the region; 10^7 as a part of the country; 10^8 as the country; 10^9 as the continent; and 10^{10} as the planet.[3] These frameworks are, in the end, only convenient and arbitrary constructs, and one can reconceive them in numerous ways to suit the situation more effectively. Building a frame around a geographical site, for instance, ignores the fact that we now interact within communities that are not tied to geography, and many of our friends and coworkers are now network based, distributed across the globe. So the frames might serve more conceptual ends, as they could span from the user, to the conversation, to the thread, to the chat room, to the platform, to the network, and beyond. It's also worth noting that this is an anthropocentric implementation of the conceptual frames, as they prioritize the human and its collectives over nonhuman ones (microbes, insects, plants, or animals, for instance). What might the sliding scalar frames look like if we focused instead on the level of the cell, the microbe, the organism, the rock, the plant, the reptile, the biome, the ecosystem, the bioregion, the planet, or the atmosphere? Exploring the issue of waste in densely settled environments, for instance, ought to take into consideration the flies, rodents, raccoons, deer, and bears that are now intimately connected to our own trash habits; one could argue that many of our climate challenges result from precisely our tendency to ignore these nonhuman points of view.[4] Scalar framing can provide a flexible approach for maneuvering through layers of complexity to identify overlooked opportunities, stakeholders, constraints, collaborators, and new viewpoints, but if it is adopted uncritically it can also embed bias and narrowness of vision into every successive vantage.

In order to explore the efficacy of scalar framing, it will help to start with an example that illustrates its adaptability: If we wanted to make bicycling easier in a location like New York City, for instance, how and where would we start? Bicycling provides a healthy, safe, efficient, and sustainable means for mobility in the city. It has multiple knock-on, positive effects for urban contexts, from public health to environmental air quality and noise abatement. However, for a variety of reasons in the United States, urban bicycle riding rates are lower than they are in other parts of the world, particularly parts of Asia and Northern Europe. A city like New York City provides additional complications, though, because of its reputation for careening cabs and belligerent buses, not to mention the unfriendly winter weather. According to the Worldwatch Institute, "The share of all trips made by bike varies greatly among countries. Chinese cities still register some of the highest cycling rates in the world, despite growing consumer interest in private automobiles. In the most cycled cities, such as Tianjin, Xi'an, and Shijiazhuang, the bicycle accounts for more than half of all trips. In the west, the Netherlands, Denmark, and Germany have the highest rates of cycling, ranging from 10 to 27 percent of all trips. This compares with about 1 percent of trips in the United Kingdom, the United States, and Australia."[5] New York City already boasts a world-class subway system and other forms of mass transit that serve the millions of commuters every day. Still, cars clog the streets and bicycle commuting is not for the faint of heart, despite recent improvements in the city's bicycle infrastructure.

If our aim is to increase bicycle riding in New York City, how might we use the scalar framing approach to identify strategies that open up the problem in new ways? For the purposes of greater specificity, we will run through the bicycling scenarios from the perspective of a designer, though one could come at this challenge from any problem-centered perspective (such as engineering, policy, business, medicine, social work, and so on). It starts, not surprisingly, at the level of the individual.

10^1

Borrowing the framing strategy of *Powers of Ten*, let's consider how a designer might increase rates of bicycle riding at 10^1, or the level of the individual.[6] For many individuals, the bicycle itself is both an encumbrance and a disincentive to use. Heavy, ungainly, and difficult to carry, the bicycle frame and messy components (as they are currently configured) make it difficult to bring them up stairs, easy to steal, and a challenge to bring on mass transportation. If designers could rethink bicycles themselves to make them more easily foldable or compact, lighter weight, theft resistant, and more pleasant to ride, more bicycle users might opt for human-powered transport instead of for fossil-fueled ones. While the past few decades have seen remarkable innovations in bicycle form and technology, not enough of those have translated to the commuter bicycle in a way that has radically transformed people's image of bicycle commuting. Lightweight, foldable scooters have occasionally made inroads into the bicycle market, but their presence on public streets is still limited. Similarly, small, foldable bicycles have also spiked in popularity, but they have not made a substantial dent in overall, human-powered commuting patterns. So, at 10^1, we might say that this is a product design problem: *If designers could create bicycles that are better suited to the commuting lifestyle and its constraints, we may well see more people willing to give up cars and mass transit and shift over to bicycles.*

Fig. 30. *Scalar framing at 10^1.*

10^2

If we zoom out one power of ten, to 10^2, to the level of the building, the sidewalk, and the street, the evident dynamics and disincentives of bicycle riding emerge. A city like New York City is simply not built for mass bicycle ownership or ridership. Apartments are tiny by comparative U.S. standards, and residents often subdivide these or share them. Storage is precious, though many more buildings are adapting to increased ridership and offering basement level bicycle storage. The sidewalks themselves are ill suited to mass bicycle parking. The city's first bike-share system, Citi Bike, required the appropriation of on-street parking and the development of high-tech corrals to accommodate even a modest number of bicycles. At 10^2, then, the problem changes from a product design problem to an architectural design problem: *How do we retrofit the city—as built—to accommodate substantially larger populations of bicycle commuters and their bicycles?*

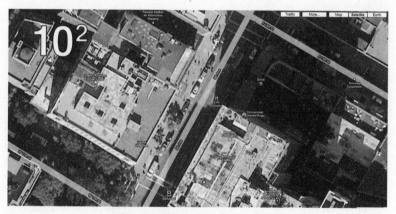

Fig. 31. *Scalar framing at 10^2.*

10^3

At 10^3, the buildings and sidewalks recede into the background and we encounter New York City's famous grid of streets and avenues. What leaps out to any bicycle rider in the city is that on the streets of New York the automotive—car or bus—is king and the bicycle is an afterthought at best, or a "nuisance" at worst. The streets were designed to facilitate maximum automobile flow, and only recently has the city recognized the needs of bicycle riders by opening bicycle lanes alongside the automobile lanes. Many cities have now gone so far as to move the lane of parked cars away from the sidewalk to create a buffered bicycle lane, a configuration now prevalent in New York City. The streets of New York are engineered for four-wheeled traffic first and pedestrians second. The avenues are wide enough that an enterprising taxi driver with a river of green lights can easily attain speeds of forty to fifty mph or higher on busy, pedestrian-lined streets in the country's most densely populated city. This free-for-all is compounded by the delirious diversity of human- and other-powered modes of transportation that currently crisscross the city and its sidewalks: Rollerbladers, skateboarders, horse-drawn carriages, motorcycles, Vespas, pedicabs, hoverboards, unicycles, and whatever else inventive New Yorkers dream up to speed their way to work. At 10^3, then, the problem is no longer a product design or an architectural design problem but has shifted to become an urban design challenge: *How can we reimagine the urban streetscape to better accommodate human-powered transport, and how do we make those changes in ways that don't disrupt all vehicular traffic and worsen conditions in the meantime?*

Fig. 32. *Scalar framing at 10³.*

10⁴

Zoom out one power of ten further, and we can now see most of Manhattan, inviting us to consider how we might generate more bicycle riding at the scale of the borough itself. In 2013 New York City launched Citi Bike, its initial foray into a shared service of bicycle provision. Cities across Europe and the United States had already experimented successfully with bike-share systems that allow riders to pick up one of a shared fleet of bicycles in one neighborhood and ride it to a station near their destination where they could then drop it off. Rarely are these systems self-leveling, however; typically, municipal employees in large trucks are redistributing the bicycles from one station to another during slower times or at night so that certain stations aren't empty while others have no space to park and lock the bikes. For the user, the service must be easy to understand, vandal resistant, weather resistant, low on repairs, attractively priced, appealing to both one-day riders and everyday commuters, safe, dense enough to make it convenient, and accessible in many languages (to make it appealing to foreign tourists). At 10^4, then, the problem shifts to a service design challenge, one that various bicycle share services have met with varying degrees of ridership and financial success: *How can we create shared systems of resources that accommodate diverse populations with vastly different needs and capabilities that is affordable, convenient, low on maintenance, and easy to use?*

Fig. 33. *Scalar framing at 10^4.*

10^5

New York City is not just one city but a sprawling metropolitan area that crosses into the nearby states of New Jersey and Connecticut. A dysfunctional, patchy system, the various transit authorities that serve daily commuters—the Metropolitan Transit Authority, the Port Authority Trans Hudson (PATH), the Long Island Railroad (LIRR), Metro-North, New Jersey Transit, and Amtrak—do not play particularly well together. At 10^5, the suburban bicycle commuter needs this regional patchwork of municipal and state authorities to work seamlessly together: She may ride her bike from her house in suburban New Jersey to the PATH train, take the PATH train into Pennsylvania Station, use a different swipe card system to take the subway into Brooklyn, and then ride her bike the final mile to her office. Along the way, she must navigate the different rules, regulations, and equipment that allows, or doesn't allow, a commuter to carry a bicycle with her. As complicated as this is—and at 10^5 we see that this becomes a systems design problem—many people choose this option to lower their daily commuting costs, minimize their environmental impact, or simply avoid the aggravation of bridge and tunnel automobile transport. The fragmented nature of the various transit authorities requires not only a vantage broad enough to see the benefits of more smoothly integrating these systems, but also enough political muscle to bring these changes to fruition. What entity will unite these fragmented systems and whose interest will they serve? *How can we design incentives for bicycle commuting across the metropolitan transit authorities in ways that increase public convenience, health, and safety while decreasing its fragmented complexity?*

Fig. 34. *Scalar framing at 10^5.*

10^6

At 10^6 New York City is a tiny dot on the map of the eastern seaboard; Washington, DC, now comes into visible range. At this almost national scale, we might ask a question about the policy role that the federal government could play in supporting bicycle transit in cities. Or we might ask the more obvious question, given its history, of why the federal government has so heavily subsidized automobile transit to the detriment of most other means of transportation—rail, buses, and bicycles. Many would argue that the global rise in the twentieth century of the "American way of life" is due in no small part to the transformative impact that the roadway system had on our patterns of settlement, property ownership, consumption, and overall lifestyle. The interstate roadway system is the envy of many nations (particularly given the enormous geographical size of the country) and a marvel of twentieth-century engineering. Publicly funded highway infrastructure propelled General Motors to become the largest corporation in the world by the middle of the century, with Ford and Chrysler not far behind. But the rise of the "big three" also meant that they exerted outsize influence on public policy through intense lobbying efforts. This explains, in part, why the United States has such an underwhelming interstate train system (Amtrak), a hybrid, public-private entity that is forever one pen stroke away from disappearing. Bus, trolley, and other transit systems in cities are woefully underfunded compared to those in other modern countries. A love affair with the owner-occupied automobile is now as much a part of the American cultural DNA as baseball and Apple and pie. This means, in part, that the potential for far-reaching and visionary urban planning that prioritizes nonautomobile transportation and embraces bicycle ridership is, at this scale, a policy design issue: *How can we reorient public policy and special-interest-group spending away from single-owner automobiles and toward human-powered forms of transportation?*

Fig. 35. *Scalar framing at 10⁶.*

10⁷

At 10^7 we have now zoomed out to the point where we must question whether any solution to the challenge of bicycle riding in the city is not itself also bound up with issues at a global scale. If we were all to own bicycles, for instance, what becomes of the global footprint of bicycle resourcing, manufacturing, and production? What metals and materials are necessary to sustain this level of production? What is the environmental impact of that industry? What are the working conditions like for those who are working in the mines and factories? How to distribute the wealth that results from the mass production of bicycles? And what political regimes are we propping up through the traffic in these materials and goods? *How might we reorient the production of bicycles toward*

local resources and contexts so that a growth in bicycle manufac-
turing does not induce environmental and political degradation
elsewhere?

Fig. 36. *Scalar framing at 10⁷.*

It would be easy to become paralyzed in the infinite
regress of questions that arise across the many scales. Every
local challenge is, at the same time, enmeshed in a complex web of influences, making it agonizing to address even
small-scale, local conditions without also confronting the
larger-scale constraints. This exercise in scalar framing risks
turning every modest problem into a global, wicked problem.
But the point of scalar framing is not to suggest that anyone
with the will to influence the conditions on the ground will
have to come up against the full force of global dynamics.
Scalar framing gains its strength from the fact that as systems
grow or shrink in scale, new opportunities emerge. Just as a

glass of water becomes a vaporous plume at its boiling point or a homely caterpillar becomes a resplendent butterfly with enough energy, problems shape-shift and transmogrify as we slide up and down the scales of the system—revealing new opportunities along the way.

There are, then, four lessons to take away from each act of scalar framing:

1. *Every local problem is likely also a global one:* There are very few local issues today that are not, at the same time, directly linked in some way to global forces that are exerting new kinds of pressure on local contexts. It would be foolish to suggest that *all* problems are global. The systems that comprise everything from local politics to pollution to violence to finance to zoning to education and to infrastructure have roots in local soil, but their topmost leaves and branches are often caught in the wires of global systems and politics. And even when problems do not reach a global scale, they do often have national or regional origins. The bottom line is that it is borderline negligent to see problems only for what they are in their most obvious or explicit forms. Reframing the problem by scale is, instead, an opportunity to discover a new point of leverage that might have seemed invisible at one scale.

2. *Act at the scale that maximizes your own capacities:* For a bicycle maker who doesn't have access to other stakeholders in the bicycle community, the best means of intervening in the

system might well be to redesign the bicycle. The impact may be more limited but, nonetheless, it may tip things in the right direction and catalyze other kinds of changes to occur. But for a bicycle enthusiast who rides together with friends on the weekends who are also involved in local politics, then perhaps focusing on questions of advocacy and policy with a politician friend may be a more strategically effective path to follow. A bicycle rider who is also a political advocate may bring local and professional insight to the political problem that few politicians otherwise possess. That collision of worldviews could provide the spark and the opening to shift the dialogue and illuminate fresh directions forward.

3. *Insight can come from reframing your problem at a different scale:* We all suffer from what systems designers call bounded rationality. It is not possible to know all parts of the system equally well, and we also cannot know the motives and actions of all participants in that system. As a result, our knowledge of the overall situation is always limited and bounded; we act rationally on that limited, bounded information, but that rationality is compromised by the things we don't even know that we don't know. By shifting perspectives and scales—to that of a bus driver or a traffic engineer or a city councilwoman—we not only gain greater empathy for their experiences, but we also open up new vantages for ourselves to see from. Donella Meadows suggests: "Change comes first from stepping outside the limited information that can

be seen from any single place in the system and getting an overview. From a wider perspective, information flows, goals, incentives, and disincentives can be restructured so that separate, bounded, rational actions do add up to results that everyone desires."[7] But even more powerfully, placing oneself in another's shoes and understanding the larger or smaller context of action from that perspective can generate new insights and ideas that may not otherwise be evident. And it certainly beats banging one's head over and over again against the same wall.

4. *Each new scale brings new possible collaborators:* The simple act of rethinking a problem from a different scale also brings into focus new actors and stakeholders who may become essential collaborators in the process. A bicycle designer may never imagine collaborating with a bus driver, but that bus driver (who may also ride a bike on the weekends) could have insights into visibility, sharing the road, traffic engineering, and bike-on-bus commuting that the bicycle rider may never have access to otherwise. Or working with an agency that is launching a bike-share service may encourage a bicycle designer to look at other precedent services in other countries, thereby revealing cultural alternatives that might have gone unexplored. Moving one's thinking across scales opens up the process to new stakeholders, increased empathy, alternative strategies, and, most hopefully, new ways of engaging old problems.

Scalar framing is not a solution itself, but a method for revealing new ideas and new collaborators when a creative problem-solving process is stuck in a rut. The process of scalar framing obliges us all to slide conceptually across a wider gamut of scales, while identifying new possibilities that we might not have noted before. It forces us to see the problem more empathetically—through others' eyes—and it can strengthen a process through the identification of new stakeholders and strategic collaborators as well.

———

Acts of compassion, generosity, or altruism can change lives, but they may not necessarily nudge systems in the right direction, despite the genuine, positive emotions that they generate. The recycling of plastic beverage bottles to create synthetic fleece was a rare success story in ecologically driven fashion retail, but we have since discovered that those microfibers are leading to a new, confounding challenge. Because they are able to be spun so thin, when they are laundered the fibers have the capacity to slip through water treatment filters and into our waterways, contributing to a new and very different environmental catastrophe whose scope we are only beginning to comprehend—no good deed, it seems, goes unpunished. For an individual, confronting the chaos of uncertainty with every small decision one faces can be paralyzing: Is taking a car on a two-hour trip to another city more environmentally responsible than taking a train, for instance (not to mention the doubts that arise as to whether the cacophonous research one finds online is, itself, trustworthy—another symptom of scale). And who has two hours to immerse oneself in the research in order to make that determination?

Moreover, in our everyday lives few of us have the capacity to think and act at multiple leverage points. Paper versus plastic? Car versus train? Less expensive supermarket produce versus organic, high-priced farm-stand vegetables? Take a job or go into deep debt for college? Most of these everyday decisions leave us lost, alone, and facing a thicket of conflicting paths forward. It is possible, however, to reverse the polarity of scalar framing, so to speak, in order to think through the consequences of individual acts and decisions. We might describe this as a form of scalar ethics, where we use scale as a decision-making framework to navigate varying degrees of certitude, risk, and impact. When we act within complex systems our knowledge will always be partial, but that realization can effectively guide our behavior if we think *through* scale.

As we confront these smaller decisions, we can use the units of the scalar framing—the individual, the family, the neighborhood, the community, the city, and so forth—to think through the options and estimate the impacts and the risks. At each scale the quandary is that the balance between certainty and risk of impact will shift. Thought of in a different way, we can draw concentric circles of immediacy in order to determine at which scale we feel our actions best fit with our moral and political values. Each larger scale—each concentric circle outward—means that the impact of our actions spreads across a greater field of impact while the risk of negative externalities also rises.

For illustration purposes, let's imagine a thirty-two-year-old shop owner who lives in Newark, New Jersey. Her business is successful, but she can see the impact that the struggling public school system has not only on her small business, but also on her customers who are struggling to get their children out of the cycle of poverty. She has no children of her own, and it would be easy to blame the problem on others, but the glaring impact of the city's civic shortcomings haunts her. She wants to get involved, but if Mark Zuckerberg's mountain of money didn't help, what could she possibly do?

- 10^1—**The Individual.** Evidence suggests that systemic solutions may be ineffective with this issue, so she decides to limit the degree of impact that she has, but to make certain that she has an impact. So, she decides to start volunteering at the local public school and tutoring at-risk children. She can start with just one student, and there is a direct correlation between the action she takes and the impact on that child—she can see him grow in confidence and capability. This may not solve the larger issue, but there's no arguing that she is having a positive impact.

- 10^2—**The Family.** While she knows tutoring can have a positive impact, she also recognizes that a child at school may not thrive without robust family support, something that can be a challenge for financially strapped families. She decides instead to serve as a "big sister," mentoring a third grader and providing the family unit with another responsible adult who can help to steer the young student toward success.

- 10^3—**The Neighborhood.** While the impact she can have on one child and her family is rewarding, she'd like to think that there are things that she can do to affect more than just one student, and so she offers to volunteer in her neighborhood middle school. Helping to conceive and paint a playground mural, cleaning classroom windows, keeping the grounds litter free, and occasionally serving as a classroom volunteer all contribute to a better learning environment and, hopefully, help students feel better about going to school. Her actions certainly impact an entire cohort of middle school students, but does it really have a measurable impact? At this power of ten, she impacts more students, but will it really make them more successful?

- 10^4—**The Community.** She starts attending citywide school board and school district meetings. Having become familiar with her local middle school, she can now advocate for its needs, but she also starts to recognize that its needs must be balanced with those of neighboring schools, which face different challenges. She begins to see the problems as systemic, rather than unique to the school she volunteers in. Her aim, at this scale, is not to mentor individual children or beautify the building and grounds, but to help shape policy—something that could affect scores of students for many years.

- **10^5—The City.** Frustrated by her local middle school's constant need for maintenance, she decides that she's going to do something about it and run for the school board. In this way she can begin to address the larger, systemic issues that seem self-evident. But as the scale changes…the problem changes. At this scale, the issue is no longer the well-being of a community of students that she has come to know well, but the tensions between the local schools and the district-wide administration, for instance. Stale arguments around state-wide, mandated tests, accountability, teacher seniority, and the role of the teachers' union come to the fore. Decisions made and actions implemented at this scale affect thousands of students—for better or worse.

There is no question that there is good work to be done at each of these scales. But each larger scale—each concentric circle outward—means that the impact is potentially greater, but also less evident and higher risk. In the end, the value of thinking through scales is to understand that as the scale changes the problem changes in nature. In some cases, the certainty of the small positive impact can outweigh our ambivalence about whether we're actually doing the right thing at a larger scale. Certainty and scale of impact appear inversely related. By thinking through scale we can balance the known with the unknown, the immediate with the distant, and the risk with the reward. There is no one "right" scale to operate at, but we can slice through any problem to reveal the sets of possibilities and the shape-shifting nature of problems themselves.

———

A frame can be a comforting device, organizing the chaos around us into a neat "box" that aligns with our worldview. Until it doesn't. Scalar framing presupposes a vantage point from which we can observe a scene and capture it in full resolution—like the Eameses' camera effortlessly gliding upward toward the heavens. It is tempting to suggest that the camera is, in fact, a neutral observer, but cameras and their views are never quite that. Nothing is neutral, and the scalar framing method is evidence of that. The scene that the camera frames in *Powers of Ten* is an index of both inclusion and exclusion. The scalar framing trap is to equate one's bird's-eye view with reality. Instead, we must recognize that the camera lens—and by association our own vision—is never unmotivated or innocent.

The seduction of the Eameses' graceful camera movement can, however, also be deceptive. Framing and focus establish the initial shot and determine what we see but also, ultimately, what we don't see. How might we have read *Powers of Ten* differently if, for example, the establishing shot had focused on her face instead of his? Or what if the film had framed a Black or mixed-race couple on a picnic rather than a White one? Or been situated on the south side of Chicago, the vast forests of the Amazon, or even the battle-scarred rice paddies of Vietnam? Underneath the cool surface of *Powers of Ten* roils a politics of what's not shown... of power, perspective, visibility, and agency. Who is framing? Who is choosing? What counts as content and context? What is left out beyond the frame?

How we frame each power of ten says as much about our own view of the world as it does about the world that we are viewing. It embodies our privilege, our power, and our politics. What we elect to keep in the frame and what we decide to exclude is not just an innocent act of free will... it reinforces our own point of view. We cannot escape our own internal frames just as we cannot escape our own shadows. But we can, at least, acknowledge their boundaries and try to displace them.

Charles and Ray Eames, by situating their camera where they did (in Chicago) and how they did (magically veiling the technology that supported the impossible drift upward and then down and inward) created the illusion that the camera is simply a technical observer of reality. But scalar framing also presents an opportunity to widen and resituate the frame... to try to make it more inclusive, representative, or even off-kilter. Each shift in perspective is also a moment to reflect upon the limits inherent in our own framing of the world around us. Scalar framing can prompt us to seek out other frames, including the frames of others. How the shop owner frames the issues of the struggling school district may be radically different from the teacher, the janitor, the principal, the parent, or the student herself. If we are not self-critical we unavoidably frame our world through the lens of our own ethnicity, class, gender, age, size, ability, and even relative clarity of vision. Recall, to a five-year-old a teenager is "old" and a summer is almost endless. The concept of parallax in physics reminds us that a shift in the relative position of the viewer will change the relationships among the objects viewed. We are not obligated to adopt the "neutral" trappings of the Eameses' objectifying eye. In fact, we are compelled to resist that. Breaking the frame of familiarity and reframing along the view lines of others will instead shatter the expected and illuminate new spaces of possibility.

Chapter 07

The Middle

How can we scale good ideas in ways that don't simply reenact the same thinking that caused the problems in the first place? If we want to put a dent in the massive problems that we have created, we will need ideas and solutions that can alter the course of thousands, millions, or even billions of people's lives, not to mention our global climate.

To think at that scale, we'll have to reimagine how we create services, infrastructure, policies, products, or even communities. We are impressively capable of solving small-scale problems, especially when the context is knowable and factors are few. We stumble, typically, when we need to solve problems that become complex and where we cannot know everything there is to know. To tackle challenges of a much larger scale, it would certainly be valuable to enlist as many stakeholders as possible into the process. "Given enough eyeballs, all bugs are shallow," goes the expression from computer programmers. More eyeballs will allow others to see into blind spots and to fill in gaps in knowledge and experience. But more stakeholders plus more participants can equal a complicated, burdensome process. Things can grind to a halt as differences in perspective and opinion collide.

What models can we draw upon as we try to scale up solutions in a complex world? There have been two predominant models of large-scale systems change: top-down and bottom-up. I will propose a third way—scaffolding—that hovers in a middle zone between these two models. In order to fully grasp what is different about scaffolding, it is first necessary to zoom in on the characteristics of top-down and bottom-up frameworks.

Top-down structures are nearly ubiquitous in human affairs. When we need to make something truly enormous in scope and scale, we typically resort to organizational logics that rely upon functional hierarchies. This is how we have built powerful armies, sturdy bridges, and the vertically integrated corporation. In these models, authority, agency, and expertise reside at the very top of the hierarchy and, in effect, trickle down to the bottom. The further down in the hierarchy one sits, the less autonomy. The task is divided up into branching sets of smaller tasks that are themselves divided further into specializations and smaller units. This was, of course, the particular genius of the industrial revolution and the assembly line and the great innovation of management science.

Top-down models assume that expertise for solutions exists at the top (company heads, project managers, policy experts, military leaders, and so on), where those "experts" can assess and evaluate the entire global problem, determine market demand or audience need, and offer a targeted solution that can scale to many. In manufacturing, for example, producers aggregate the resources necessary to procure the materials, fund the tooling, and ship the finished goods to the consumer's door; in policy worlds, experts study the issues, talk to other experts, develop policy, and then pass that policy as regulation or laws that shape our behaviors and attitudes.

Top-down systems are very effective for some things, and not so great for others. The advantages of top-down systems are:

- A top-down system can scale ideas and decisions quickly because it requires the input of only a few, elite decision-makers.
- Upper-level managers can break apart complicated challenges into smaller, simpler component parts that are easier to manage and that they can recombine back into an effective whole.
- There is oversight over the entire process; someone can see the big picture to make sure that redundancies and inefficiencies are mitigated.
- Decisions can be made rapidly because consensus is not essential.

- There is not a great need for deep intelligence and fore-sight at the lowest levels—simply operationalizing ideas from above is sufficient.

But top-down systems struggle because:

- Communication primarily flows downward within the system and true feedback loops are rare.
- They are vulnerable to attack because removal of the top can cause aimless drift or a loss of coordination and command.
- The solutions are one size fits all (or most times S, M, L, and XL) and do not adapt to changes in the user base.
- There is inertia in the system because decisions bottle-neck at the highest levels.
- Insights and decision-making are taken away from those closest to the "facts on the ground."

This last point is especially noteworthy. Because top-down systems centralize strategy and expertise at the top, at a level furthest from the producers and consumers, actors in these systems often lose touch with those who have the most direct experience of the products or services or policies. The system is simply not designed or equipped to adapt to divergent needs. Tools are a classic example of this inflexibility: They are designed to suit right-handers but not the left-handed, or the able-bodied but not those with arthritis or disabilities.

Top-down organizations put inexpensive, quality scissors into the hands of many, but that doesn't mean that they addressed the needs of all equally well. The advantages that top-down organizations have when it comes to scaling quickly are offset by their inability to be responsive to the highly specific needs of all their diverse user groups.

Bottom-up systems (sometimes called *self-organizing* or *emergent*) are rarer, and hence a bit more exotic. They have not dominated the landscape of business and organizational production, though this is starting to change. Bottom-up schemes are more common in biological systems, and that itself gives us a clue as to their properties and their capacity for resilience and sustainability. In natural selection, for example, there is no master planner—no supreme authority or intelligent designer—that is directing the path of evolution of the behavior of agents. Mutations happen on the edges of the system that lead to new hybridities (or innovations), which can then either positively or negatively affect a species' ability to thrive. Those traits that lessen the viability of the organism's capacity to reproduce its genetic line are selected against, while those that enhance reproduction and survival are selected for. As the agents share those traits (through reproduction), new traits are absorbed into the DNA of the species. There is no overarching plan that, for instance, foresees an advantage for humans to lose their tails. One's fit within a context determines the winning and losing traits, and the agents collectively iterate through successive alterations...until better fits emerge. Natural selection is a slow-moving, often arbitrary process that takes remarkable amounts of mutations, produces enormous numbers of failures, but slowly and ineluctably generates "solutions" to the problem of thriving in an ecosystem. This resilience is a trait that we would do well to mimic.

In contrast to most industrial manufacturing processes, the do-it-yourself (DIY) movement recognizes that expertise is not limited to the expert class. Typically, the movement relies upon open standards, knowledge sharing, and amplifying communication among its members. Most DIY producer-consumers don't aspire to the same economic dominance model that conventional, market-driven producers do (though the retail sales platform Etsy is changing that dynamic). This bottom-up approach is solutions oriented, but not in a way that presumes market scalability (and that often rejects it for ideological reasons). The thriving subculture of IKEA hackers, for example, delight in repurposing the multifarious parts of an IKEA product (or products) and recombining them into functional or even subversive new kinds of furnishings—turning IKEA's Billy or Expedit storage systems into litter boxes in disguise, for instance—and then openly sharing them online at sites such as https://www.ikeahackers.net. There is not a greater scheme at play in this system, and market control is not the objective. A thriving community may be.

Many of the properties that bottom-up systems embody are, in fact, antithetical to—or at least run counter to—policy or industrial production processes. In bottom-up systems the individual agents operate with little global knowledge of a preordained final product or objective of their collective work. Each assay is an experiment—an iterative small-scale, low-resource sketch of a solution that works in that particular context but may not work for another. For larger-order, macro-level intelligence and solutions to emerge from bottom-up processes there must be robust and active information flow, links, and feedback loops so that incremental advances can be shared across the network and within a community. What makes bottom-up systems so astounding is that no matter how smart and perspicacious its agents are, they do not know—and cannot know in advance—to what ends their mutations will lead. There is an almost magical quality to them. Adaptive solutions emerge from the intercoordinated behaviors of the many—each trying and failing and trying and succeeding and trying and failing again.

Bottom-up systems may not typify the most vivid cultural monuments of human creation, but they do lead to highly stable, resilient, adaptive, and even intelligent system behavior. The advantages of bottom-up organizational structures are:

- Local actors have agency, autonomy, and power; hierarchies don't predominate.
- Simple rules plus simple agents can yield surprisingly coordinated and complex behaviors.

- The system is highly responsive to local conditions and contexts.
- Because no executive authority is controlling the group, the organizational structure is less vulnerable to catastrophic failure.
- The system is self-optimizing and self-regulating.

The principal disadvantages of bottom-up systems are that they are very slow to scale and cannot be programmed, so to speak, to seek out specific goals or larger objectives. Evolution takes a long time and follows its own meandering path. The goal-seeking behaviors of the swarm must emerge organically from the coordinated behaviors of the many, so these systems are both process heavy and slow to respond. They are stable and resilient over time, but they do not respond to top-down directives or incentives.

If top-down systems are rigid, hierarchical, swift, and require leaders, and bottom-up systems are resilient, adaptable, slow-moving, and egalitarian, then can there be approaches that graft the best of each onto something that is neither top-down nor bottom-up?

So we stumble, finally, into the middle. Most of our most vivid life experiences are situated at one extreme or the other—all or nothing. We lose interest in the in-between because it seems to hold none of the inherent tensions that the extreme ends do. But there is a case to be made for the middle, and in the conceptual landscape of systems from simple to complex, the middle turns out to hold most of the mystery and, perhaps, the greatest potential for rethinking how we scale insights and good ideas. Zoom into the middle and we find mutants, hybrids, and crossbreeds within this often-overlooked ecosystem.

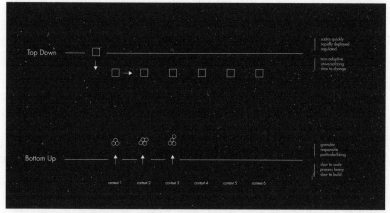

Fig. 37. *Top-down and bottom-up processes.*

We tend to believe that newness comes from nothing, ex nihilo, but in fact the new almost always springs from mutations in the existing. Only since the modern era have we sworn holy allegiance to the myth of the new. The unanticipated is always already there in the middle...waiting to emerge. So rather than ping-pong back and forth in an endless volley between top-down and bottom-up, perhaps it is time to find a middle way between them. If scaling is a process that does its work between the small and the large or the one and the many—between an instance and its generalization—then what lives in the middle?

———

What would an approach to scaling good ideas look like if it leveraged the middle? What is a process that exists in between the idea and its realization as a finished outcome? If we were aiming to grow roses, to use an analogy, we might design and build a lattice so that the roses have an infrastructure for successful growing. The aim is for the roses to flourish and for the lattice, ultimately, to fade into the background. One does not build a lattice for the sake of a lattice, but as just enough structure so that the roses may flourish. Similarly, a scaffold does not make the building itself, but it needs to be envisioned so that the building may take proper form. When the building is done, the scaffold disappears. Whether we call this a scaffold, a lattice, a platform, a culture, an infrastructure, a framework, a schema, or a rule set, the intent is the same: to design an intermediary framework that is not the thing itself (that is, the rosebush), but the means by which many different configurations (or roses) may emerge. The aim is not to create a single idea multiplied, but to nurture the conditions of possibility for diverse results to emerge.

What makes this mesolevel, scaffolding approach a hybrid of top-down and bottom-up frameworks? It is top-down because someone must design the process itself, just as they would the scaffold. And scaffolds can take many forms, depending upon the output that one envisions: simple, complex, antic, ambitious, ornamental, irregular, outrageous, or risk-averse. To design the scaffold does require some knowledge and an awareness of process. But it is bottom-up because one should design the development process so that it maximizes, optimizes, and synthesizes the ideas of many. It must capture the wisdom of the crowd and the granularity of those who know the most about its actual impact. There must be channels for feedback and pathways for iteration that allow the outcome of the process to develop according to an internal logic that will not be evident from the outset. This means working and reworking interventions periodically over time, listening to the participants, adjusting the program, fine-tuning the approach, and iterating continually. And there must be constant feedback loops that reconnect the scaffold makers to the community.

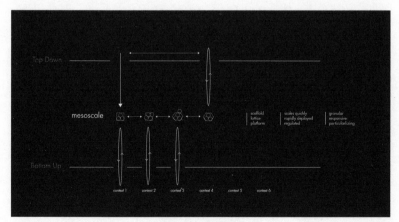

Fig. 38. *Scaffolding.*

The challenge is to design protocols so that many can contribute to collective creation and decision-making processes without simply swamping the process in further chaos. Wikipedia, for instance, uses a highly elaborated set of protocols for updating, editing, and posting its crowd-sourced entries. Without it, controversial entries would quickly devolve into the wiki-equivalent of editorial shouting matches. Digitally enabled networks certainly help to make recursive structures that are responsive to many, but they are not the only means of tapping into dynamic reservoirs of energy and ideas. Festivals, workshops, and make-a-thons also mobilize and motivate people in good old-fashioned, face-to-face situations. What is lost in speed and efficiency is more than made up for in the ways that subtlety, nuance, collaboration, and negotiation play out in face-to-face human encounters.

Scaffolding: How to Start?

How does one develop a scaffolded process? An open and responsive process may not always obey the following sequence of steps, but one can usually find most of these in any successful project:

1. **Attunement: The more the merrier.** The aim, in this phase, is to listen, process, learn, and mirror the community's thinking back to itself as a project plan. Ultimately, the goal is

to establish common ground and to empower all participants to recognize that they have a stake in the outcome and a role to play in shaping it. This is a process of delimiting the problem space collaboratively, regardless of who originates the problem framing itself. It is also an opportunity to identify key stakeholders who will be part of any process of boundary setting.

2. **Ideation: Glimpses of the possible.** There are no silver bullets. Making insights, dreams, fears, and worries material and visible will begin a process of creating consensus around the directions for the project. The ultimate objective of collaboratively generating ideas is to envision a range of possible futures that could be brought into being. As Linus Pauling famously quipped, "The best way to have a good idea is to have a lot of ideas." The cogeneration of strong, bold visions for future states will create open potentialities and multiple possible outcomes. The results will be cogenerated possible futures. They will be states of play. The "solution" then becomes a program, or an unfolding set of conditions that, with community input, feedback, and energy, evolves to fit the shifting context.

3. **Prototyping: Envisioning together.** For solutions to emerge, one must put into play scripts for action that the community can pick up, adopt, adapt, transform, put down, reconfigure, remake, and ultimately make their own. The aim during this phase is to make things fast, cheap, temporary,

and provisional. The objective is not a solution per se, but animated feedback. What we might call the law of successive approximation pertains at this phase: Each successive prototype must be qualitatively less wrong than its predecessor. Or, as programmers say, fail early and fail often. The goal is to use the provisional prototypes to surface feedback. The challenge is to know when to stop specifying and when to turn the scripts into fixed outcomes.

4. **Programming: Create the conditions of possibility.** What gets produced must take the lightest form possible. It is a collective call to action and the delimitation of a place to stand from which new possibilities are imaginable. It is a scaffold. Or a platform. Or a program, in the many senses of the word. What it is, as a thing, is not all that important. What it can enable is more important than what form it takes. It cannot be overbuilt with stylistic bravura and ornamental gewgaws. Agreements, contracts, visions, charters, commitments, relationships, and tactics for moving forward: The innovator's job is to structure this ensemble of capacities so that they are iterative and evolving. The scaffold is only the condition of possibility. Once its job is done it will recede into the background, just as a lattice gives way to blooming roses. The hand of the designer may be more present in this phase.

5. **Recursion: How the scaffold learns.** Proliferation is the means by which small ideas scale. Recursion is the means

by which good ideas learn. Can the design of a path forward for one community translate—or scale—to another? Yes, provided that there are multiple sets of feedback loops happening simultaneously. First, the originating community must be actively and formally incorporating the shortcomings they have experienced and the hacks that they improvised back into the platform and tools themselves. The platform must evolve. Second, once shared with others, there must be traffic in innovation back and forth between the communities and their respective platforms. In other words, feedback loops have to exist in all directions at all times. This requires the creation of a communication infrastructure that can grow, manage, and sustain the crosscutting flows of insight, critique, and information that the platforms' use generates. The platform establishes the conditions by which multiple communities can cross-pollinate.

6. **Feedback: Consumption as regeneration.** Consumption, in a scaffolded process, is not depletion but regeneration. It is more akin to climbing up a tree or swinging from a tree branch than it is cutting down a tree and turning it into a paper bag. What does consumption look like in this system? Consumption is not the acquisition and depletion of a limited resource, in this instance, but the interaction with a constantly renewable one. The system is self-balancing, like an ecosystem. Rain becomes water becomes sustenance becomes waste becomes evaporation becomes rain becomes

water. Because the platform is a condition of possibility, it is a continual source of regeneration. Each new idea expands and evolves the platform while also feeding back insights to it. Feedback, literally, means providing nourishment back to a source, and each use of the platform replenishes it and its restorative capacity.

Clearly, there are aspects of both bottom-up and top-down strategies in this process. There is a role to play in designing the conditions of possibility for things to emerge, but one's touch must be light, deft, and tactical—just enough structure. The real objectives are to accelerate this emergent process and to speed the cycles of iteration, feedback, and learning. Only in this way can the process reach scale at a pace that mimics constantly diverging needs. There are some lessons, learned from the perceptual and conceptual behaviors of scale, that can guide the process:

- Don't design the solution. Design a scaffold for finding the answer.
- Expertise is out there.
- Make uncertainty into an asset—there is no other condition beyond it.
- Relinquish control by shifting it to others.
- Incentivize and equalize participation over time.
- Make consumers into producers.
- Establish robust channels so that communication flows in all directions.

- Design a process for selecting features that work and deselecting those that do not.
- Make sure that the feedback reaches all the way to the edges.
- Minimize the scaffold over time.

There is, thus, a delicate, almost Zen-like state that one must achieve between control and letting go, between setting things in motion and letting them wander where they need to. It is a process more akin to gardening than it is to design.

———

While it may be tempting to suggest that scaffolding is a pipe dream, an abstract construct without grounding in reality, there are examples of the process in the world. While they may not map perfectly onto every aspect of scaffolding, the parallels are instructive. They also illuminate both the risks and possibilities.

An operating system is the bedrock upon which applications such as Microsoft Word, the web browser Firefox, Outlook, or Photoshop run, and housed inside of that operating system is the kernel, the essential code base upon which other, additional features and operations sit. According to some estimates, Microsoft's Windows 10 operating system contains 50 million lines of computer code, and it still is the operating system that runs on the majority of personal computers worldwide. That staggering number represents a scale of human effort and intelligence that is almost unthinkable (though Google's code base, *Wired* magazine reports, is orders of magnitude larger—two billion lines of code).[1]

Linux is open source software that functions as an operating system on computers and other electronic devices. Linus Torvalds, the person for whom Linux is named, launched the Linux kernel in 1991 when he was a graduate student at the University of Helsinki. This was still an early stage in the development of desktop computing, and while there were already desktop computers on some people's desks, most still considered a home computer a relative oddity (and the World Wide Web, as we know it today, was still years away). Torvalds was working with Minix, a stripped-down version of the operating system Unix, but he found that it didn't meet his particular needs. He set out to create the kernel for a modification of Minix instead. He had reached out to Andrew Tannenbaum, the creator of Minix, with suggestions for changes, but Tannenbaum was unreceptive to the suggestions. Torvalds, then, set out to write a new kernel that could, at the same time, be open to the contributions and suggestions of others.

What makes Linux different, though not unique, is that Linus Torvalds developed a scaffolded model of source code production that leveraged the contributions of others to ensure its success. It distributed the potential for development, expansion, and refinement, while also creating an infrastructure for participation and feedback that harnessed the energy of thousands of stakeholders. The process that Torvalds (along with others) oversaw did not emerge fully formed on the first day of the project's inception. It grew and evolved as Linux itself did. Nor does it represent a pure form of egalitarian cooperation, as some would like to believe. In fact, that is what makes it particularly illustrative of a scaffolded process. It grafts aspects of a top-down model of production to bottom-up participation. The canniness of Torvalds's approach, however, was to recognize that once he had built the collaborative infrastructure for Linux, the project could scale up without a top-heavy organizational structure. As of April 2019, the Linux operating system consisted of 24 million lines of code, all humming along in concert like a finely tuned orchestra.[2]

To write tens of millions of lines of code and to make all of the various functions embodied by the source code interact smoothly is akin to building the George Washington Bridge over the Hudson River or sending a rocket to the moon. Any small defect can bring the whole thing to a grinding halt, and the potential for those overlooked errors scales as the project does, or at times even faster. When Linus Torvalds first released the Linux kernel to the world in 1991, his approach was distinctly different. "I'm working on a free version of a Minix look-alike for AT-386 computers," he wrote in an email that announced his intentions. "It has finally reached the stage where it's even usable (though it may not be, depending on what you want), and I am willing to put out the sources for wider distribution. . . . This is a program for hackers by a hacker. I've enjoyed doing it, and somebody might enjoy look-ing at it and even modifying it for their own needs.... I'm looking forward to any comments you might have."[3] There is little indication in this email that Torvalds was fully aware it was a scaffolded system that he was launching, and he's doing not much more here than sharing the fruits of his labor with a community of like-minded hackers, hoping that someone else might find his work useful.

But what started as a shrewd gesture quickly evolved into an ecosystem that drew other programmers to it. By 1994, when Torvalds released Linux 1.0, the number of voluntary contributing programmers had bulged to seventy-eight, hail-ing from twelve different countries.[4] Recognizing the remark-able growth, effectiveness, and evolution of Linux, Torvalds and his collaborators, by necessity, forged an infrastructure for collaboration that maximized both the utility of the sys-tem and the voluntary energy of the operating system's pro-grammers. What made Linux such a runaway success was that the developers were able to conceive and design a plat-form for participation that, simultaneously, acknowledged the contributions of anyone who donated their work, managed the infernal complexity of the mushrooming source code, and established channels and loops for feedback that were robust and resilient. Perhaps most critically to the health of the source code, they instituted three key strategies—or simple rules— that encouraged participatory energy while minimizing bugs:

Each subroutine was modular, meaning that it could both stand on its own and plug in to the larger matrix; programmers had to test the viability of their own products and survive a "check-in" to ensure they weren't introducing bugs into the larger system; at any point, anyone could "fork" the code to create an alternate branch if that suited the programmer better than contributing to the mothership. These rules, combined with those of an innovative licensing scheme (the GNU General Public License, which enforced the requirement to distribute freely), created a weirdly fertile territory for explosive but ordered growth.

As an apparently bottom-up production process that scaled up remarkably quickly, the organizational structure of Linux is not, as many mythmakers suggest, that of pure chaos and radical egalitarianism. Its success stems from the optimal but tenuous balance that Torvalds and others created between top-down administration and bottom-up autonomy. Much of how it came into being is the direct result of the system of production that Torvalds envisioned, but that does not at all mean that what Linux is results directly from Torvalds's work alone. To the contrary, it is an aggregation of the coordinated contribution of thousands of programmers. But what we can recognize in this process is the finesse by which Torvalds leads a design process without controlling the content or context. Instead, he sets wheels in motion. As he wrote in a post to the Linux mail list in 1992, "Here's my standing on 'keeping control,' in 2 words (three?): I won't. The only control I've effectively been keeping on Linux is that I know it better than anybody else."[5]

As Linux grew in scope and complexity, Torvalds was faced with a simple problem of scale: The size of the code base was getting too large for any one person to oversee. This is commonly known as the "Linus doesn't scale" problem. Understanding his own limits, he created an inner circle of lieutenants who could oversee subsections of the code. So it is certainly the case that the management of Linux's growth took on forms that resemble a more orthodox, top-down organization, but that also simply reinforces the fact that the Linux production model was neither purely flat nor wholly hierarchical. The responsibility of these lieutenants was not—and this is a critical inflection—to determine the direction of the code's development. Instead, their role was to ensure that the code itself was agile, effective, modular, and elegant. The point is that the level of complexity of the project required that an infrastructure of collaboration develop that was equal to the task of compiling millions of lines of code without squashing the astonishing, voluntary energy of the contributors.

Part of the genius of this open source production model is that it blurs the distinction between consumers and producers, turning every participant into a potential consumer of the source code but also a potential creator of it. While the Fordist model of production presumes a stark, categorical difference between the two groups, this scaffold model undercuts it in novel ways, leading to tighter bonds within the producer-consumer community and strengthening the system of production. As a producer-consumer, the programmer has a vested stake in the quality, durability, and the efficacy of not only what she produces, but what others do as well. This is what generates the community. And the social organization, conversely, is what creates the robustness and resilience of the end product itself. It is also certainly the case that when people invest their time and energy into the creation of a product, they are less eager to toss it aside for the next shiny, new bauble.

What does this all add up to? How has an open, mesoscale process competed in the marketplace? This operating system, which emerged from the aggregated efforts of volunteer programmers, has captured the largest portion of the web server market; it is the basis for the Android operating system, which is the most popular operating system in the world; it lives in the majority of netbooks and all Chromebooks; and runs in roughly 98 percent of the supercomputers made.[6] These are statistics that would make Microsoft—a company that has paid its programmers tens of billions of dollars over the same amount of time—green with envy. And in March 2016, Microsoft more or less capitulated to the success of Linux by allowing its own database management software, SQL Server, to run on the Linux operating system.[7] Miraculously, a process that is distributed, open, and completely voluntary has somehow managed to outpace in multiple categories a crown jewel from one of the world's largest private corporations.

While not a perfect model of scaffolded innovation, the platform development that led to Linux illustrates many of the characteristics of the scaffold process. Moreover, it demonstrates that the model can generate spectacular outcomes, even if there are qualities to Linux that may not be transferable to other processes (the infinite, no-cost reproducibility of code, for instance). How do the two models line up?

- **Attunement:** In Torvalds's opening post, he writes, "This is *a program for hackers by a hacker*. I've enjoyed doing it, and somebody might enjoy looking at it and even modifying it for their own needs.... I'm looking forward to any comments you might have" (italics added). In other words, he demonstrates his understanding of the culture of hackers and open source programming, and has invited others to voluntarily share in the pleasure of solving problems for themselves or for others. He has given something away for free—or built rapport—and what happens next is open to many possible directions.

- **Ideation:** Torvalds opens his post with this vision: "I'm working on a free version of a Minix look-alike for AT-386 computers." In this opening he has built a vision for what is possible: free software with no strings attached, though it is limited and potentially buggy.

There's a possible future embodied in the invitation, but it can be realized only through the participation of many others.

- **Prototyping:** Embedded in Torvalds's opening post is a vivid sketch of the system of production: open source code, iterability, feedback channels, and the promise of wider distribution. The alignment with GNU GPL, which came a year later, established a framework for copyleft, or the right to distribute, fork, and share infinitely. The Linux community then later instituted the lieutenant structure to speed up the process of product evaluation as the code became more complex. The model that Linux has become was not there from the very outset, but through a slow and iterative evolutionary process it eventually self-selected a form.

- **Programming:** Together, the attributes of open source code, iterability, feedback, and the infrastructure of check-ins comprise the platform upon which Linux thrives. Linux is not simply the latest distribution of its source code—it is not a designed *thing*. Instead, the most recent distribution is the end result of a scaffolded framework that creates the conditions of possibility for the base code to emerge. It is dynamic and, in some ways, alive. Linux continues to evolve without any single individual orchestrating the direction. Torvalds may coordinate it, but he does not shape it. His efficacy is dependent upon the thousands of contributions of programmers and users who continue to push into directions that Torvalds could never have foreseen.

- **Recursion:** One of the more remarkable aspects of Linux's development is the means by which millions of lines of code are voluntarily generated while also being modularized, distributed, reconnected, and reassembled over and over again. And it works. A sophisticated mechanism of "pipes" and "ports"—basically a Tinker Toy–like structure that allows programmers to break off subcomponents to tinker with while the structure of reassembly remains intact—keeps the total machine running. Lieutenants can identify a bug in one subcomponent such that it won't compromise the whole. Like the liquid metal cyborg from *Terminator 2*, each module can dissolve into a puddle of lines of code but then be reassembled back together again better and stronger than before. Improvements ricochet through the system, bootstrapping the source code along the way.

- **Feedback:** Users do not simply consume Linux, they also remake it. And none of this could happen without the complex channels for feedback and feedforward that Torvalds and others established for the process. The flow of effective communication is the lifeblood of Linux. Comments written into the source code, posts on usenets and blogs, and even heated arguments, trolling, and flamewars all contribute to the information ecosystem that keeps Linux alive and, ultimately, adaptive.[8]

The continuous flow of information in all directions—vertically but also horizontally—ultimately renders the system and process transparent and knowable to any who stumble into it. Just as anyone interested in the history of a Wikipedia entry can trace it backward and forward and render its development visible, the documentation and flow of communication in the Linux ecosystem keeps the process open and knowable to all.

Linus Torvalds and others certainly played a role in shaping the coming to being of Linux, but they did not make it. Instead they made it happen. This may seem like some sly bit of semantics, but the difference is important. There is intent in the creation of the scaffold for the emergence of Linux, but that same design intent was not what generated twenty-five million lines of code. There is a dynamic balance between top-down and bottom-up that animates the code itself—brings it to life. While it may not be a true, thriving ecosystem, it bears a strong resemblance to one. It is dynamic, adaptive, and resilient. It scales up innovation while resolving complexity.

Scaffolding embodies a paradox: It is both designed and open. Evolving, complex, nonauthoritative, and recursive, this mesoscale process blends together qualities from both technical and biological systems. It maximizes social participation by creating thriving assemblages of productivity, communication, and adaptation. It is experimental in the way that life itself is experimental: There is no guarantee that any single innovation or mutation will survive in its local eco-system. Instead, many small assays must happen in parallel, and knowledge and insight must circulate freely and openly across the whole system. Not fully biological, not fully technological, but ultimately powerfully social. Not top-down or bottom-up...but something that thrives in the rich, loamy middle. Fixing a broken planet, untying the knots of our political system, or making our society more just will not be business as usual. It requires both the willingness to embrace radical uncertainty and the trust to invite others to help discover the solution.

Chapter 08

Feral Pigs and Wicked Problems

Paralyzed by overwhelming complexity and adrift in the mists of scalar changes, we are often at a loss to know how best to move forward. Whether we're in the checkout line choosing between paper or plastic or we're at the office overwhelmed by email, the options seem inadequate. The environmentalists' mantra "Think global, act local" suggests one model of large-scale change: If change agents everywhere focused attention on their local contexts and sustainably fixed those problems, these actions would collectively color in the dots in the map of the world, turning a dismal picture into a brighter one. There are some fundamental issues with this model of change, however. The critique, known in population theory as the Netherlands Fallacy, focuses upon the fact that solving things locally may, in many instances, mean creating new problems elsewhere. In other words, welcome to the networked, wicked world. Anne and Paul Ehrlich's

1990 book *The Population Explosion* brought the Netherlands Fallacy into the popular imagination. They focused on the Netherlands, in part, because a *Forbes* magazine article had suggested that overpopulation was not a problem and pointed to the Netherlands as an example of a state where overpopulation and high standards of living could coexist. The Ehrlichs see this differently: "It is especially ironic that *Forbes* considered the Netherlands not to be overpopulated. This is such a common error that it has been known for two decades as the 'Netherlands Fallacy.' The Netherlands can support 1,031 people per square mile only because the rest of the world does not."[1] The Netherlands, in other words, is able to maintain a high standard of living precisely because the country exploits through imports the relatively low cost of food and energy in other parts of the world. They have acted locally (to maximize their well-being and ecological footprint), but by solving for their local impact they exacerbate inequalities and asymmetries elsewhere.

The "scaling" theory of change operates differently. Rather than people everywhere turning inward to face their local problems one locale at a time, a scaling theory of change suggests that a singularly innovative idea can cascade across multiple locales, gaining economies of scale in efficacy, energy, and time. This model assumes that there are shared qualities to the challenges that can be addressed by a single, innovative model. The ability of community policing to stem the precipitous rise in violent crime in a few cities, for example, meant that many cities across the country adopted that same model with the hope that they would see the same outcome, despite any local differences. Similarly, the rise of bike-sharing services, pioneered in European cities to address ecological, traffic, and health challenges, led to a wide-scale proliferation of these services in other cities that were looking to manage this same assemblage of urban problems. The scaling model of change works in ways that are analogous to viral infections or forest fires. The model assumes that change will take hold in context B because it has worked in context A and because context B is primed—has the necessary, analogous conditions—for the thing to spread. But scaling implies something more than just diffusion of the idea. The leap from one host community to the next in the process also involves a ratcheting up of the size and complexity of a solution. The problem with this approach, however, is that it lacks the continuous feedback loops of scaffolding. This model implies that scaling operates only in one direction—up—and not bidirectionally like scaffolding. The scaling model of innovation won't learn and adapt along the way if the only goal is to sell more, reach more, or convince more.

To scale something up (that is, scale as a process and not a framework) implicitly raises the question of how to intentionally change systems, or how to start something small and then grow in size to meet the needs of a broader, more diverse community. It is a process that is as relevant to social innovation as it is to business or technological innovation. A community in a rural village may discover a way to address public health that is low cost and lasting, and public health officials at a regional or national level may urgently need to implement that innovation across a much wider population. A small garment design and manufacture business may reap the benefits of a great press review or a viral tweet, and need to ramp up production and invest much more capital faster than they intended, while recognizing that that significant uptick of demand may not sustain itself perpetually into the future. Or a home-sharing service, such as Airbnb, may launch successfully in a few locations, but how does it grow into a massively scaled platform that can manage not only millions of users but also the varying rules, regulations, and cultural customs around home sharing and hospitality in countries as diverse as Saudi Arabia, Senegal, and Singapore? Is there something we can learn about scaling that can act as a guide or plan and work for all different contexts? The short answer may be no, but the longer answer reveals some surprising insights about scale and system change.

To design, plan, innovate, or even act at scale is to swim in the ocean of systems: complex, fluid, dynamic systems. Systems are combinations of elements and relationships that, collectively, demonstrate particular behaviors. Systems can be physical (like model train sets or the weather) or they can be immaterial (as in religious beliefs, families, or software). Not everything is a system, but most things are part of some sort of larger system.

A wiring diagram for a toaster, for instance, represents a simple, engineered system; with some instruction most of us could likely understand how it works (when an actuator is pushed, electrons flow in this direction, causing these wires to heat up...and so on). Historically, system thinking emerged from the disciplines of engineering and computer science, though traces come from the social sciences as well. Engineers have been responsible for creating remarkably complicated systems that perform in astonishing ways (airplanes that safely fly, skyscrapers that stand tall while swaying securely in the wind, bridges that can span chasms, the always-on internet). Comprised of thousands, if not millions, of parts, what typifies these systems is that they are linear, which means that one can identify with a great degree of specificity what every single part does, how it contributes to the whole, and how to repair it if the system fails. Software such as operating systems and word processing applications are also examples of complicated systems, comprised of tens of millions of lines of code, all of which must interact harmoniously for us if we want our work to progress unerringly. One small bug, one small piece of misbegotten code, can hamstring the system; it takes only the repair of that line of code to get things back up and running.

Complex systems, on the other hand, are neither simple to comprehend nor simple to fix. In a complex system there are no straightforward solutions. Small, targeted inputs do not yield outputs knowable in advance. The relationships are non-linear, meaning that there is not a one-to-one correspondence between an element and its role within the larger complex. Also, we cannot deduce the relationships between elements from the system itself. Small perturbations may have next to no impact at one moment, and an outsize, transformative impact at another—this is the riddle of complex systems. The scaling model of innovation works well within linear systems, but tends to fail catastrophically within a nonlinear, complex system because simple inputs rarely lead to predictable outputs.

Take the example of wild pigs in the rural Southwest. Aggressive, omnivorous, with seven-inch tusks that can tear open flesh, this predator is wreaking ecological havoc across rural land with little to stop its explosive growth and destruction. It is smart, able to outwit hunters and game wardens alike, making it a prized adversary for hunters on the prowl for a stiff challenge. And that, in some ways, may explain why the wild pig is suddenly flourishing in Southern states. An overview of the invasive pigs' habitats reveals that its random settlement pattern is most likely the result of hunters releasing the pigs into the wild; these are not native habitats. The pig's intelligence and evasiveness make the hunting of it a thrill, which is why hunters introduced it into the wild initially in the United States. Experts now estimate the total population to be between two and six million hogs, scattered across thirty-nine states. They reproduce prodigiously, with a female producing up to twenty-four piglets each year, and they have no known local predators, except for human hunters.

Most significantly, this invasive species' proliferation threatens the health and resilience of human-engineered and natural ecosystems across the South. "Hogs erode the soil and muddy streams and other water sources, possibly causing fish kills. They disrupt native vegetation and make it easier for invasive plants to take hold. The hogs claim any food set out for livestock, and occasionally eat the livestock as well, especially lambs, kids and calves. They also eat such wildlife as deer and quail and feast on the eggs of endangered sea turtles."[2] While the various species that make up the pig population have existed for centuries, it is only since the 1980s that the numbers have ballooned. Invasive wild hogs cause an estimated $1.5 billion of damage nationally each year, and controlling the population is beyond the capacity of hunters or fish and game officials—they are simply too crafty, too numerous, and too fertile to eradicate.[3] Few hunters could have foreseen that letting loose a few wild pigs for the purposes of sport hunting would upset the fragile balance of these ecosystems. As the saying in the Southwest now goes, "There's two kinds of people: those that have wild pigs and those that *will have* wild pigs."[4]

Such is the volatility of complex systems: Small inputs can unleash out-of-scale results. And these complex systems surround us. While we may be able to fathom complicated, engineered systems by breaking them down into smaller component parts, complex systems defy logic and rational means-ends calculation. All of the good intentions in the world won't turn a fussy, complex system into a predictable, complicated one. This is a syndrome that Horst Rittel and Melvin Webber glimpsed and artfully described in their increasingly influential 1973 essay, "Dilemmas in a General Theory of Planning." Coining the expression *wicked problem* to describe a new class of unsolvable social complexes (*wicked* in the sense of infernally complicated, not malevolent), they profile the emergence of these "dilemmas" against the backdrop of the rise of the professional planning classes. Wicked problems, such as gun violence, traffic congestion, or poverty, have several alarming features: They only seem to get worse when we attempt to solve them, there is no end to them, and they have no boundaries—each wicked problem is typically the symptom of another wicked problem. Poor health is a symptom of poor schools. Poor schools of chronic unemployment. Chronic unemployment of high levels of crime. High levels of crime of high levels of violence. Violent neighborhoods are correlated to poor health outcomes. And around and around the wicked problems go. How do we address crime without looking at economic opportunity, but how do we address economic opportunity in a job market that requires higher levels of education? The irony for planners is that they actually solved many of the problems that were plaguing cities in the developed world during the nineteenth and twentieth centuries. Systematic, rational planning rooted out most of the social ills of the early twentieth century in cities: Paved roads created interconnectable regions, housing projects sheltered even the poor, modern water and sewer systems eradicated disease, and public schooling gave children an opportunity to move up the economic ladder. So what happened? In a word: complexity.

The very nature of the problems changed, from the manageable and the predictable to the wild and wicked. Challenges that used to yield to carefully thought-through, rational solutions do so no longer. Instead, the problems have phase-changed from the complicated to complex. They have taken on unexpected and unmanageable characteristics, or behaviors, that do not resolve neatly, as the earlier class of problems seemed to. In other words, as the systems changed in scale, they manifested new, unanticipated behaviors. Multiple factors have induced this new state of affairs, but three in particular are relevant for our discussion here. First, systems within social contexts have social repercussions. That is, the messy interconnections between diverse communities' needs, wants, capabilities, politics, resources, and opportunities evade simple, straightforward intervention. What works for one group of people may not work for a different group, because these social systems are unbounded, "open," and internally conflicting.

Second, the challenges of the early twentieth century required planners to be *effective*, whereas these new classes of problems require the solutions to be *just*, according to the needs of the affected communities. Keep in mind, the authors were writing in the shadow of the late 1960s, when various rights movements (gender, ethnicity, sexual orientation, and ability) were insisting that the scales of justice had historically tipped toward one privileged group in particular. Solutions that had seemed right and just to a ruling cadre of white male elites might not sit so well with increasingly empowered, though chronically underserved, communities. Robert Moses might have felt that putting an expressway through the South Bronx made planning sense to those well-heeled car commuters heading to leafy Connecticut suburbs, but the expropriation of Jewish and African-American residents from their neighborhoods to make the Cross Bronx Expressway certainly did not feel right or just to them.

And third, conventional planning assumed that the planner could sit outside of the system and gaze down upon it with an all-knowing, bird's-eye view of the system. But no experts can actually gain this vantage, or be independent of the systems they observe. "The expert is also the player in a political game," they write, "seeking to promote his private vision of goodness over others'. Planning is a component of politics. There is no escaping that truism."[5] For Rittel and Webber, there were no ways to slice through the Gordian knots that were tying themselves in the second half of the twentieth century. The professional class of planners, of which they were members, could only ever lay claim to partial knowledge and only ever truly embody the values of a narrow subset of actors.

To make matters even worse, complex systems have become even more entwined and entangled since Rittel and

Webber wrote their essay in the early 1970s. As the world has become even more interconnected, the knots become knottier. The problems are so tangled that there is not even an obvious beginning, middle, or end of the thread to unwind and follow. Have the world's problems become too complex to navigate? Are the social, technical, and environmental systems that we interact with every day too tangled and gummed up to ever become manageable? How do we navigate this profound complexity—or, to put it slightly differently, how can one act in the face of complexity?

Systems are everywhere around us: they are technical (the telephone system), social (our network of friends), and environmental (the storm water that flows across our city streets). They range in scale from the global (the internet or the weather) to local (a compost pile or a car). Systems are comprised of elements that are interconnected and that collectively display behaviors and even, at times, a higher purpose. With systems, the whole is greater than the sum of the parts. Perhaps inspired by the rise of ecological thinking, which helped us to see ourselves as critical but irresponsible parts of global ecosystems, it's nearly impossible now to look at things, processes, and phenomena and not see the systems that they are parts of. This explains why we so frequently read and hear about "broken systems." We actually *see* systems more clearly, but their behaviors can still be mysterious.

We already know that human systems and natural systems interact in infinitely complex and counterintuitive ways.

Farming, for instance, or animal husbandry has always represented the human struggle with unpredictable biological systems. Add to that tangle the technical systems that are now global in scale and near instantaneous in their capacity to carry multimodal forms of information, and we begin to understand why our problems have become so wicked. We often convene the best and brightest together to solve our biggest problems, but the solutions oftentimes cause more damage than good. For instance, our shift from incandescent to compact fluorescent to LED lightbulbs has created a dramatic increase in energy efficiency. Now, however, the low cost of LED lights has led to an overall increase in their installation and usage, precipitating a global increase in quantities of light pollution.[6] Nonlinear, complex systems do not respond proportionally to changes. Small inputs can lead to cascading changes (such as when a few algae from other bodies of water metastasize into lake-killing algae blooms), and huge inputs can lead to little impact (think of Mark Zuckerberg's massive influx of resources to the Newark school district). Given this randomness and unpredictability, how do we not become paralyzed by the idea that any one of our actions might lead to an unequal and inapposite reaction?

The twin devils of uncertainty and complexity are not insurmountable obstacles, but what is necessary is not just more force applied in the same direction—a bigger hammer for a bigger problem—but a new mind-set and a whole new angle of embrace. Donella Meadows, a cerebral and poetic systems thinker, maintained the position that systems, even complex systems, had leverage points, or opportunities within a system where the application of pressure or force or intelligence or resources could fundamentally tip the system toward more optimal behaviors. Much like scalar framing, each leverage point provides a qualitatively different opportunity to nudge systems in more optimal directions, like an acupuncturist's needle deftly applied to a suffering patient. But there are hazards that lurk within our desire to plan, control, and manage systems that do not, by their very nonlinear nature, yield easily to these tactics.

This command-and-control mind-set is a legacy of a mechanistic worldview: that if we just apply enough force or intelligence we can engineer the systems states we want—like replacing a blown-out fuse in an electrical system—so that everything just flows smoothly again. As with the Eameses' all-seeing camera, there is a temptation to equate one's own view of a situation with an objective view of it, and to assume that the right action to make a change is the action that seems self-evident. But if this were the case, then we wouldn't have wicked problems. There is a much deeper problem to think through, that of knowledge itself: "We can never fully understand our world, not in the way our reductionist science has led us to expect. Our science itself, from quantum theory to the mathematics of chaos, leads us into irreducible uncertainty.... If you can't understand, predict, and control, what is there to do?"[7] Despite the temptation to puppeteer systems, complex systems are inherently too unruly for such control schemas. At the center of every hard-to-crack complex system and wicked problem is a gooey mass of radical uncertainty.

Rather than being overwhelmed by the scale, complexity, or messiness of the problem, we must adopt Zen-like engagement and active attunement. It is not mastery of systems that we should seek out, but a higher awareness. "We can't control systems or figure them out. But we can dance with them!...I had learned about dancing with great powers from whitewater kayaking, from gardening, from playing music, from skiing. All those endeavors require one to stay wide awake, pay close attention, participate flat out, and respond to feedback," writes Meadows.[8] Each of these is an activity that engages the mind, the body, and the senses in a dynamic push-and-pull. Attunement is not just our eyes glued attentively to the computer screen. It is a reassertion of the primacy of the body in coordination with mind as a means to embrace complexity more humbly and more fully. It is the body, mind, and senses present to the situation.

There is no one-shot, silver bullet, magical answer. The entangled systems of our moment look much more like biology than physics, more like complex ecosystems than wiring diagrams or computer code. But we also glimpse here the outlines of a subtly different method—a different angle of approach that recognizes that the combination of scale and complexity demand new and alternative strategies. We must have the patience to engage over and over again and the attentiveness to do so in very small ways. It is an iterative process of some failure mixed with some success (solve and re-solve, design and redesign).[9] The data and learning that comes from this will fuel any forward trajectory—recursive loops of feedback and adjustment, probing and withdrawal, assaying and reflecting, humility and inspiration, listening and acting. It is a method of successive approximations—each subsequent iteration reduces the error and increases the forward momentum toward some sort of (unreachable but aspirational) steady state. Or Zeno's paradox: never quite getting there but at least getting closer.

But who is doing the designing? It cannot be just experts, and it must be all of us. Here again is where scaffolding plays a role: We must all be fully engaged in a well-designed process that encourages our participation, draws upon our local wisdom, and defies the distant experts. When autonomy, agency, and the capacity to change systems is handed back to those who use the systems we've created, we will finally start to see a more nuanced and responsive set of behaviors. Expert-driven, top-down solutions are brittle; they do not empower but pacify. Scaffolded approaches build resilience by connecting us all up into intelligent and responsive participant-builders. We must create the conditions for a dexterous application of openness, receptiveness, attunement, new frames of reference, and the dogged persistence to design and design again and again and again. Small, nimble, recursive, and scattershot designing may not necessarily more quickly evolve a complex system in the right direction, but at least its self-correcting tendencies will overcome the temptation to give the system one big push...in the wrong direction.

———

Hans Monderman was the closest thing there's been to a celebrity traffic engineer. In 2008 when he passed away from cancer at the age of sixty-two, his modest and unorthodox ideas about traffic engineering were ricocheting around the world of traffic and urban planning, and even seeping into the broader culture at large. Features about him and his work appeared in the *Wilson Quarterly*, *Wired*, the *New York Times*, and the *Guardian*. Monderman's built work is not extensive, but the reputation of the Dutch traffic savant within the traffic cognoscenti is. His ideas are small perturbations that have had outsized effects. To demonstrate the safety and functioning of his traffic redesigns, Monderman used to perform a trick for his interviewers while taking them on walking tours of his handiwork: He would close his eyes and walk backward into an intersection he redesigned. He always emerged unscathed. To understand why he would demonstrate his ideas' effectiveness this way, we have to understand how he enabled us to dance with the systems.

Traffic engineering, like most engineering, works in fairly linear ways. The size and complexity of solutions tends to scale with the size and complexity of the problem. The town of Drachten, in the Netherlands, with a modest population of forty-four thousand, hired Monderman in 2001 to address a poorly functioning intersection in the town center where automobile traffic had resulted in the deaths of two children.

Fig. 39. *Intersection in Drachten, the Netherlands (before). Photo: Eddy Joustra, © Municipality of Smallingerland.*

Delays were frequent and accidents not uncommon. A typical response by a traffic engineer would have been to add more and better signage, better-regulating stoplights, and bollards and sidewalk curbs to protect and divide the drivers and pedestrians. In other words, if you've got a bigger problem, you need a bigger hammer. Monderman, however, went in a radically different direction: He removed almost everything from the intersection. He eradicated almost all of the signage and stoplights; he brought the cafés and pedestrians closer into the street; and he eliminated curbs and installed more public artwork. The results of this radical experiment in traffic chaos: Traffic flow increased by 30 percent while accidents decreased by 50 percent.

Monderman reframed the situation, thinking at the level of the individual driver rather than the engineering plan. He also embraced uncertainty, realizing that in some cases it is better to empower others to navigate complexity than it is to hold their hands through it. Monderman's philosophy, which has come to be known as "shared space," reframes traffic in terms of the agency of the pedestrian and the driver rather than the automobile and the transport system. We might say that he thinks at the scale of 10^1 rather than, say, 10^3. Or, in Monderman's words, "If you treat people like idiots, they'll behave like idiots."[10] Monderman realized that traffic signals and signage had been progressively turning drivers into passive actors, reliant upon instructions from the paternalistic infrastructure around them. By this logic, more traffic meant more infrastructure, which produced more passive drivers, which produced worse results. By shifting his attention from the automobile to the driver, he made drivers and pedestrians equals in the dance of the intersection and active negotiators rather than passive followers.

Monderman perceived traffic as operating at two distinct scales. As Tom Vanderbilt writes, "Monderman envisioned a dual universe. There was the 'traffic world' of the highway, standardized, homogenous, made legible by simple instructions to be read at high speed. And there was the 'social world,' where people lived and interacted using human signals, at human speeds. The reason he didn't want traffic infrastructure in the center of Drachten or any number of other places was simple: 'I don't want traffic behavior, I want social behavior.'[11] By removing as much signage as possible and adding a grassy knoll to the center of the intersection, thus bringing pedestrians and others more directly in spatial conflict with cars, Monderman was counting on drivers and pedestrians to adjust their ways from passive observation of controlling rules to active negotiation of a shared space.

Fig. 40. *Intersection in Drachten, the Netherlands (after). Photo: Ben Behnke, Spiegel.*

Monderman understood that both parties could more effectively navigate the encounter if they were empowered to do so, not managed by traditional traffic engineering rules handed down from above. By loosening up control and shifting agency to the level of the drivers and the pedestrians, Monderman risked chaos and uncertainty, but he also suspected that a choreography of active visual and social cues would emerge from the interactions. And it did. Contrast this approach to a smaller, lower-volume traffic circle in Concord, New Hampshire, population forty thousand, where the traffic engineers opted to install, by latest count, twenty-seven traffic signs in a quiet, residential neighborhood in order to help guide motorists and pedestrians through this unprepossessing roundabout.[12] Monderman's ideas have spread to other towns

Fig. 41. *Roundabout in Concord, New Hampshire.*

in the Netherlands and to Germany, Sweden, and the United Kingdom, where they have been equally successful.[13]

Monderman followed three key strategies in his rethinking of traffic: think in scales, embrace uncertainty, and put our bodies and our senses back in the picture. To do this, he created a scaffold or platform where drivers and pedestrians could cocreate their own rules of the game. A conventional approach would assume that all know-how exists with the expert traffic engineers, and that only they could resolve the problem with the virtuous application of their intelligence. Instead, Monderman recognized that distributing agency and solution seeking to the level of the individual, rather than the moving cars, would create the conditions for a better solution. It worked because the system—or antisystem—that he redesigned empowered the pedestrians and the drivers to engage all their senses in the choreography of the traffic circle.

What would Facebook or Google look like if they choreographed systems that engaged all of us in the development of privacy settings? What would our school systems look like if we built frameworks that empowered students to shape their learning environments, and those frameworks themselves learned and became smarter? How would our response to climate change differ if we took the reins from the expert policy makers and imagined a framework that gave us all a role to play and the feedback loops necessary to make a real difference? Our paralysis in the face of scale and complexity is not because we have no role to play, or no agency. That's the illusion. The current systems we have built have taken agency out of our hands at the same time that their overseers have convinced us that they have the answers. Top-down, brittle systems disempower us, though in some cases we've blithely ceded that power to them.

There is more intelligence in the masses at the edges than with the experts at the center. And there is more capacity to solve things at the local level where the problems are more immediate, provided that the problem solving is then shared back into a recursive and adaptive process. We must take the capacity back to embrace entanglement and use it to our ends.

The Participatory Budgeting movement takes budgeting decisions out of the hands of bureaucratic experts and gives it back to the people who are directly impacted. It is a process that requires some design expertise, certainly, but one where the designer creates just enough infrastructure so that those directly impacted work out the priorities collectively and iteratively...and face-to-face. Disintermediation is not the goal. Embrace uncertainty, engage with everyone, dance with chaos. Monderman shows us what it looks like when we dance directly—backward and blind—into the maw of complexity.

Chapter 09

Presence

All models are wrong; some models are useful.

—George Box[1]

We squint at windows, shuffle files around, and juggle documents and spreadsheets on our desktops as if there is nothing unusual anymore about the fact that all of these are visual metaphors for a style of working that many of us no longer participate in. And then we wonder why the rest of the world doesn't bend to our will in the same ways that electrons and pixels do. We have constructed a digital mirror, so to speak, of our work, social, and leisure environments. We spend untold hours "immersed" in these digital spaces, and yet we are really outside the glass peering in. Our shoulders slump, our necks crane forward, and our fingers skitter along a keyboard and trackpad to bring to life this ephemeral new world that we are collectively building.

The long-term effects of time spent in this environment on our bodies and our minds will reveal themselves over time; we are like the first cosmonauts, volunteering for an open-ended journey to the edges of cyberspace. In this new territory, new rules apply: One hundred percent of a letter-sized document is 5.5 by 8 inches, and a poster and postage stamp are indistinguishable in size. Despite its wonderous, empowering, and tantalizing qualities, we are still not really at home in it yet. It's as if the laws of physics don't quite seem to apply in the same ways, and our relationship to the shape and scale of things in this immaterial world is still evolving.

Scale is more than just a means for measuring things, as should be evident by now. To understand it better, we have had to look deep into its inner workings in order to find there the inklings of a new logic. The immaterial entanglements we find ourselves in will not disappear anytime soon. Hopefully, we can now see scale more clearly for what it is, a framework through which to explore these entanglements and a means by which we can articulate a new sense of the possible.

———

There has always been a slippage between the world and how we represent it to ourselves, so it's not surprising that the digital environments we have built would also not always hold up to close scrutiny. Photographs, but also paintings, drawings, and even maps draw us into their miniaturized worlds in cunning ways, inviting us to ignore the scalar sleights of hand that they perform. In "On Exactitude in Science," a short story numbering just 155 words (in its English translation), Jorge Luis Borges conjures up the scalar paradoxes built into our systems of representation and knowledge. As with many of Borges's pieces, it comes to our attention as if discovered pressed in a dusty old book in a library...a scrap of uncertain provenance. To heighten that experience, Borges starts out with an ellipsis, as if we've stumbled into the middle of an ongoing story:

> ...In that Empire, the Art of Cartography attained such Perfection that the map of a single Province occupied the entirety of a City, and the map of the Empire, the entirety of a Province. In time, those Unconscionable Maps no longer satisfied, and the Cartographers Guilds struck a Map of the Empire whose size was that of the Empire, and which coincided point for point with it. The following Generations, who were not so fond of the Study of Cartography as their Forebears had been, saw that that vast Map was Useless, and not without some Pitilessness was it, that they delivered it up to the Inclemencies of Sun and Winters. In the Deserts of the West, still today, there are Tattered Ruins of that Map, inhabited by Animals and

Beggars; in all the Land there is no other Relic of the
Disciplines of Geography.
>—Suarez Miranda, *Viajes de varones prudentes*,
>Libro IV, Cap. XLV, Lerida, 1658[2]

Ostensibly a fragment from a larger piece, *Viajes de varones prudentes* (Travels of Wise Men), this brief, poetic excursion covers miles of conceptual territory, eloquently and efficiently renting asunder our dreams of a truly knowable world.

Borges uses the parable of the map to subvert the idea that our forms of representation are capable of measuring up to our full experience of reality. Whether literature, film, painting, poetry, music, dance, or even language, these forms are all second-order approximations, or reduced abstractions, of lived experience. They do not and they cannot capture life "point for point." To do so would amount to matching the hubris of the imperial mapmakers. Casey Cep, writing on the allure of maps in literature, suggests that "the literary equivalent of the emperor's map would be a biography of everyone in the world, or a novel of every second of every minute of every day: literature, like a map, gains its power from selection, from miniaturization."[3]

Representation functions, in other words, as a kind of scale model of reality. It shares qualities and features of it, it can even look and feel like it, but it can never aspire to stand in for reality in its full plenitude. Beauty, or even our humanity, may lie in its degree of difference from reality...in the admission that the scale model or the miniature will always come up lacking. But in that gap between the thing itself and its representation there exists a world of possible magic, of human experience.

Are we all, then, lost in the map without a desert? Has the map exceeded the territory? In our "Deserts of the West," the sand softens beneath our steps, providing no sort of firm foundation. Heat shimmers off of the hot sand, deforming our vision; oases are only ever mirages. To be without markers, without guideposts, is to feel lost in a smooth, featureless landscape—a figure dissolving into the ground. For General McChrystal, the map of operations had certainly exceeded the battle. Our grasp of the world is comprised of signifiers built upon signifiers, to borrow a term from linguistics, or turtles standing upon turtles all the way down, to lean on a metaphor from mythology. This is the reason that scale is such a critical construct to wrestle with. It is buried in the heart of the very way that we come to know the world. But it is also slippery, which is why it can be hard to wrangle. It shape-shifts from being a means for measure to being a framework for acting; from a catalyst for surprising system changes to a means for anchoring the figure to the ground; and as the source of confounding challenges to the beating heart of representation itself.

If shifts in technology and networks are decoupling scale and measure from the human experience and then bending and twisting it across our digital networks, how do we adapt?

The knowable, mechanistic complications of the early twentieth century are evolving, becoming chaotic networks and ecosystems of information flows. This does not mean that we, like Luddites, should turn our backs to the entangled world we've built. Nor is this a lament for a simpler time.

In the early days of the graphical user interface, designer Bill Gaver created the SonicFinder, an audio interface for the Apple computer that ascribed auditory "weight" to the sizes of files.[4] Simple in concept, the interface relayed a higher-pitched sound when a user selected a smaller file, and a lower-pitched one for a larger file. The interface even fed back different pitches based on the amount of storage space left on a drive or disk. What is intriguing about this road not taken is that it—in a very small way—reveals to us the ways in which scale was eventually *removed* from our interfaces. Why is a one-megabyte file no different in visual size or perceptual "weight" from a one-gigabyte file? We lose important sensory capacities through our inattention to scale.

The first computer input devices were punch cards. From there, the command line became the principal means by which programmers controlled what operations computer processers could do. The evolution from the command-line interface to the graphical user interface was a paradigm-busting shift that brought modern computing to the fingertips of the masses. The visual metaphors of files, desktops, and trash cans translated an alien language of scripts and commands into a drag-and-drop environment that mimicked familiar tools. Creators of these interfaces and spaces often drew upon the laws of physics, but not always. Now, as we hurtle toward virtual, augmented, and mixed reality, new possibilities will arise to build the human body and its affordances back into our nonphysical entanglements. This should not be a return of skeuomorphic interfaces as a stylistic technique to anchor our experiences to the familiar in the digital realm (digital calendars with "leather" trim or bulging buttons with metal bevels and drop shadows). Instead, it is a recognition that we must find ways to tie our primary means of information gathering and processing to something more than just our eyes, ears, and fingertips. And we must pay particular heed to the ways in which we are remapping scale to the detriment of our own capacities to think and act. In 2012, a designer for IKEA dropped this bombshell: Between 60 and 75 percent of all product images in an IKEA catalog are fully digital constructions. In other words, they are not photographs as we have known them, but hyperrealistic, computer-generated simulations. As we adjust yet again to no longer trusting our senses, we will also find ourselves falling into these slippery traps. Journalist Mark Wilson described IKEA's wizardry this way, "In essence, Ikea is creating digital furniture at the real-world scale."[5] At this point, I hope, it should be clear enough that "digital furniture at real-world scale" is a verbal construction whose illogic fully captures the strangeness of our present moment.

Thinking *through* scale is a means for reasserting the deep relevance of the figure—the human body and its senses—as we navigate new grounds. It is an ethic, in Aristotelian terms, or a way of putting wisdom appropriately into practice.[6] Thinking *through* scale is a way of unknotting but also reknitting the figure to the digital ground, the citizen to her surround. Networked digital experiences have reconfigured our senses in ways that we did not predict. In the early days of computing, the term for the human body that programmers often used was "meat," a deadening of the body's relation to this new perceptual environment. What we must redesign is *presence*, or our capacity to inhabit more fully both digital and physical knowledge spaces in ways that we may not yet even grasp. Thinking *through* scale helps us to see that we must retune our own presence by imaginatively restitching our bodies and our social selves in more effective and creative ways into the fabric of our digital ground. The Obadikes use data to breathe human life back into data, helping us to see the destructive ways in which our machines are furthering violence and racism. Hans Monderman confronts the chaos of an intersection by putting human bodies on the same path as automobiles, and letting us risk figuring out how to thrive together.

In an attempt to put wisdom into practice *through* scale I have proposed strategies that look to retie the threads between the body, its senses, and our immaterial and entangled ground. Like David McCandless or Kara Walker, we can use images and stories to counteract the inhuman drift toward quantitative abstraction and ever bigger data. Borrowing from Charles and Ray Eames, we can develop a scalar ethic that allows us to slice through our paralysis in the face of complexity and to recognize that we do have real alternatives, even when we don't see them at first glance. Inspired by the open source community, we can design scaffolds that leverage the insights and experiences of many, rather than the narrow expertise of just a few. Most important, though, we must give up our compulsion to control and overmatch the chaos we confront and learn to embrace our complex systems in a dynamic choreography of attunement, conversation, feedback, and counteraction.

Human-created magic, miracles, and invisibilia surround us all the time: At any moment we are inundated by animating waves from radio, cellular, and Wi-Fi networks—not to mention good old electricity—but we don't even take notice. They effortlessly and miraculously bring our environments to life, though we may not yet fully understand their impact on our brains and our climate. Perhaps, in the future, our human sensorium will evolve or expand to meet this new horizon: We may eventually ingest data, smell fishy networks, and see through complexity to a deeper truth.

The surprising inner workings of scale can break instruments and unsettle us. Like complexity, scale has characteristics, idiosyncrasies, and patterns. It subverts, destabilizes, and surprises. We cannot force scalar phenomena to bend to our will. In the era before electronics our bodies fit in our world in relatively predictable ways. No longer. The evolution from industry to information, the shift from atoms to bits, and the bewildering effect of entangled networks have collectively refigured our capacities in ways that make our old maps irrelevant. These strategies for reconfiguring presence may help to reorient ourselves in the fog. They are not the answers, but approaches for thinking through scale differently. Our attunement to scale and its tendencies will have to become even more finely calibrated. We will never master the vagaries of scale, but perhaps we can better embrace them and fold their unsettling logic into our strategies for remaking the possible.

Acknowledgments

This book project exists only because of the kind, wise, and generous support of too many people to properly mention, thank, or even fully recall. It is the product of hundreds of sideward conversations, impromptu comments, and curious questions that have pushed me to explore how to think about scale and our everyday experiences.

There have been certain figures whose insights have been indelible but whose sustained mentorship and friendship has been even more transformative for me. Each has expanded my horizon of the possible in incandescent and enduring ways: Paola Antonelli, David Comberg, Tony Dunne and Fiona Raby, Anthony Guido, George Marcus, Tim Marshall, Mike and Katherine McCoy, Jonas Milder, the late, great Bill Moggridge, Jane Nisselson, Bruce Nussbaum, Anna Valtonen, and, of course, Tucker Viemeister, who lured me into the design profession before I even knew that I might fit in there.

I've also been fortunate enough to have decades-long bonds with an astounding group of friends to whom I owe too much to describe: Jean-Vincent Blanchard, Christoph Cox,

Bruce Grant, Margot Glass, Dan Rosenberg, and Sarah Verdone (whose radiance and humor I miss every day).

There are so many amazing colleagues from so many moments of my professional life who have made this adventure both more fun and more illuminating: Patty Beirne, Rajesh Bilimoria, Ayse Birsel, Andrew Blauvelt, Ron Burnett, Heather Chaplin, Clive Dilnot, Carl DiSalvo, Fred Dust, Lisa Grocott, Hilary Jay, Natalie Jeremijenko, Colleen Macklin, Alison Mears, Miodrag Mitrasinovic, Jane Pirone, Hugh Raffles, Amanda Ramos, Mathan Ratinam, Johan Redstrom, Rupal Sanghvi, Radhika Subramaniam, Joel Towers, Laetitia Wolff, and Susan Yelavich.

For over twenty years I have had the privilege to be part of a mind-bending summer design conversation in the Rocky Mountains hosted by the inimitable Mike and Katherine McCoy. The High Ground Design Conversation has provided me not only a community to be a part of but also a rare opportunity to test out fledgling ideas to a crowd of boisterous colleagues who have always been open, warmly critical, and appropriately snarky in perfect proportion. There have been too many to name, but they know who they are.

Teaching is a thrill, particularly because I get to mix it up with bright and creative minds who chisel away at my assumptions and push my thinking further. So much of what I have written about in this book and elsewhere is a direct result of the complicated and exciting conversations I've had with now former students (who number in the hundreds) in the Masters of Industrial Design program at the University of the Arts and in the Transdisciplinary Design program at Parsons.

It is a privilege to have the time and space to write a book. Thank you to the New School for the sabbatical that led to this manuscript that led to this book. It took me longer to write the book proposal than it did to write the book itself. I never could have made it through that process without Andrew Blum and Hugh Raffles, who both shared their proposals with me when I just couldn't wrap my head around how to write one. Simone Ahuja, to whom I reached out of the blue, introduced me to her agent, who later became my agent. I will continue to pay forward the remarkable kindness that Simone showed to me. That super-agent, Bridget Matzie, never let me give up but never compromised either—until the proposal was in just good enough shape to show it to publishers. Through that process I was lucky to meet Gretchen Young, my editor at Grand Central Publishing, who has pulled this book into shape through a precise balance of insightful feedback and heady enthusiasm. Any tinny turns of phrase and all leaps in logic that remain belong to me alone. Emily Rosman, Bob Castillo, Haley Weaver, and Albert Tang at Grand Central were stellar help at crucial points in the process of getting this book to the finish line. It is better because of their work. Thanks, too, to my intrepid research assistant, Ryan Westphal, who scoured the world to help me get the permissions necessary to reproduce so many images.

I am a product of my sprawling family—over twenty-five

large and counting—and I see a reflection of each of my siblings in everything I do. This sprawling family also includes my in-laws, Millard and Jancis Long, whose active interest and questions have always pushed my thinking. My deepest debt of gratitude goes to my parents, Cynthia and James Hunt, who nurtured my curiosity and always supported my wayward, sometimes harebrained, interests. I only wish my mother were still with us so I could see her smile at the book's publication. My amazing children, Felix and Ivy, inspire me each in wildly different ways. Curious, creative, fearless, talented, smart, ethical, funny, and, most of all, deeply unimpressed with most everything I say...no parent could be luckier. And, finally, I have hitched my wagon to a brilliant, bold, and glittering star—Judith. This book would not exist without her love, support, and care. I can only hope I have returned these in kind. Big time.

Notes

Introduction. *How Much Does a Gigabyte Weigh?*

1. Cal Newport, "Is Email Making Professors Stupid?" *Chronicle Review*, February 12, 2019, https://www.chronicle.com/interactives/is-email-making-professors-stupid.
2. Michael M. Grynbaum, "Even Reusable Bags Carry Environmental Risk," *New York Times*, November 14, 2010.
3. Dale Russakoff, "Schooled: Cory Booker, Chris Christie, and Mark Zuckerberg Had a Plan to Reform Newark's Schools. They Got an Education," *New Yorker*, May 19, 2014.
4. Michel Foucault, *The Order of Things: An Archaeology of the Human Sciences* (New York: Vintage Books, 1970), xv.

Chapter 01. *On Exactitude in Science*

1. *This Is Spinal Tap*, directed by Rob Reiner, USA: Embassy Pictures, 1984.
2. Jim Dykstra, "What's the Meaning of IBU?" in *The Beer Connoisseur*, February 12, 2015, https://beerconnoisseur.com/articles/whats-meaning-ibu.
3. "What is the Scoville Scale?" Pepper Scale, https://www.pepperscale.com/what-is-the-scoville-scale/ (accessed December 17, 2018).
4. Sarah Lyall, "Missing Micrograms Set a Standard on Edge," *New York Times*, February 12, 2011, https://www.nytimes.com/2011/02/13/world/europe/13kilogram.html.
5. Quoted in Robert P. Crease, *World in the Balance: The Historic Quest for an Absolute System of Measurement* (New York: W. W. Norton, 2011), 131.
6. Crease, *World in the Balance*, 119.
7. Bureau International des Poids et Mesures, *The International System of Units*, 8th ed. (Paris: Stedi Media, 2006), 112–16.

8. As this manuscript was being completed, the 2018 General Conference on Weights and Measures declared on November 16, 2018, that after over a century of use, the platinum-iridium kilogram standard would be retired. In its place, and commencing on May 20, 2019, the official kilogram would now be defined by a universal, physical standard. "The kilogram, symbol kg, is the SI unit of mass. It is defined by taking the fixed numerical value of the Planck constant h to be 6.626 070 15 × 10^{-34} when expressed in the unit J s, which is equal to kg m^2 s^{-1}, where the meter and the second are defined in terms of c and ΔvCs." Brian Resnick, "The World Just Redefined the Kilogram," Vox, November 16, 2018, https://www.vox.com/science-and-health/2018/11/14/18072368/kilogram-kibble-redefine-weight-science.

9. Crease, *World in the Balance*, 38.

10. "Member States," Bureau International des Poids et Mesures, http://www.bipm.org/en/about-us/member-states/ (accessed December 17, 2018).

11. Crease, *World in the Balance*, 96.

12. Bureau International des Poids et Mesures, *S.I.*, 112.

13. Crease, *World in the Balance*, 223.

14. Kern Precision Scales, "The Gnome Experiment," http://gnome-experiment.com (accessed May 1, 2019).

15. J. C. R. Hunt, "A General Introduction to the Life and Work of L. F. Richardson," in Oliver M. Ashford, H. Charnock, P. G. Drazin, J. C. R. Hunt, P. Smoker, and Ian Sutherland, eds., *The Collected Papers of Lewis Fry Richardson*, vol. 1, *Meteorology and Numerical Analysis*, gen. ed. P. G. Drazin (Cambridge: Cambridge University Press, 1993), 8.

16. Geoffrey West, in his important book on the physical laws of scale, puts it this way: "In general, it is meaningless to quote the value of a measured length without stating the scale of the resolution used to make it." Geoffrey West, *Scale: The Universal Laws of Growth, Innovation, Sustainability, and the Pace of Life in Organisms, Cities, Economies, and Companies* (New York: Penguin Press, 2017), 140.

17. "International Atomic Time (TAI)," Bureau International des Poids et Mesures, https://www.bipm.org/en/bipm-services/timescales/tai.html (accessed March 30, 2019).

18. "Insertion of a Leap Second at the End of December 2016," Bureau

International des Poids et Mesures, https://www.bipm.org/en/bipm -services/timescales/leap-second.html (accessed March 30, 2019).

19. Luke Mastin, "Time Standards," Exactly What Is...Time? http://www .exactlywhatistime.com/measurement-of-time/time-standards/ (accessed March 30, 2019).

Chapter 02. *The Figure and the Ground*

1. Walter Benjamin, "On Some Motifs in Baudelaire," in *Illuminations: Essays and Reflections*, ed. Hannah Arendt, trans. Harry Zohn (New York: Schocken Books, 1969), 175.

2. Elizabeth Blair, "Some Artists Are Seeing Red over a New 'Black,'" NPR, March 3, 2016, http://www.npr.org/sections/thetwo-way/2016 /03/03/469082803/some-artists-are-seeing-red-over-a-new-black.

3. "FAQs," Surrey NanoSystems, http://www.surreynanosystems.com /vantablack/faqs (accessed March 8, 2016)

4. "FAQs," Surrey NanoSystems.

5. "How Black Can Black Be?" BBC News, September 23, 2014, http:// www.bbc.com/news/entertainment-arts-29326916.

6. "Nielsen: "Nearly Half of All Available Time Now Spent with Media," Insideradio.com, December 12, 2018, http://www.inside radio.com/free/nielsen-nearly-half-of-all-available-time-now-spent -with/article_7b988596-fddd-11e8-a4ec-9795e181ae0d.html.

Chapter 03. *These Go to 11*

1. F. W. Went, "The Size of Man," *American Scientist* 56, no. 4 (Winter 1968): 409.

2. Went, "Size of Man," 407.

3. Molly Webster, "Goo and You," *Radiolab*, Podcast audio, January 17, 2014, http://www.radiolab.org/story/black-box/.

4. Douglas Blackiston, Elena Silva Casey, and Martha Weiss, "Retention of Memory through Metamorphosis: Can a Moth Remember What It Learned As a Caterpillar?" in PLOS|ONE (March 05, 2008), DOI: 10.1371/journal.pone.0001736.

5. Jim Al-Khalili and Johnjoe McFadden, "You're Powered by Quantum Mechanics, No Really...," *Guardian*, October 25, 2014, http://www .theguardian.com/science/2014/oct/26/youre-powered-by-quantum -mechanics-biology.

6. Toncang Li and Zhang-Qi Yin, "Quantum Superposition, Entanglement, and State Teleportation of a Microorganism on an Electromechanical Oscillator," Cornell University, September 12, 2015, updated January 9, 2016, arXiv:1509.03763 [quant-ph].

7. Chris Anderson. *Free: How Today's Smartest Businesses Profit by Giving Something for Nothing* (New York: Hyperion, 2009), 12.

8. Anderson, *Free*, 52.

9. Anderson, *Free*, 154.

10. Anderson, *Free*, 128.

11. Anderson, *Free*, 161.

12. Carolyn Kellogg, "Chris Anderson's almost-'Free,' Kindle Price Drop and More Book News," *Los Angeles Times*, July 9, 2009, http://latimes blogs.latimes.com/jacketcopy/2009/07/chris-andersons-almost-free -and-more-book-news.html.

13. As if this scalar-driven economic hall of mirrors is not confusing enough, it is also important to point out that Chris Anderson himself was caught in a quite untoward scandal upon publishing his treatise on free and freedom: Waldo Jaquith, writing in the *Virginia Quarterly Review*, accused Anderson of plagiarizing content from, of all places…Wikipedia. Anderson immediately acknowledged the inappropriate citations, suggesting that it was more or less a technical error in the citation style that he and the publisher used. He claimed responsibility for the infraction, but the irony was painful. Evidently, for the pirate, the enemy is not obscurity, but the bright lights of internet popularity. Ryan Chittum, "*LA Times* Soft-Pedals *Wired* Editor's Plagiarism," *Columbia Journalism Review*, June 29, 2009, http://www .cjr.org/the_audit/lat_softpedals_wired_editors_p.php?signup=1&signup -main=1&signup-audit=1&input-name=&input-email=&page=1.

14. Kevin Kelleher, "Amazon's Secret Weapon Is Making Money Like Crazy," *Time*, October 23, 2015, http://time.com/4084897/amazon-amzn-aws/.

15. Alex Hern, "Fitness Tracking App Strava Gives Away Location of Secret US Army Bases," *Guardian*, January 28, 2018, https://www .theguardian.com/world/2018/jan/28/fitness-tracking-app-gives-away -location-of-secret-us-army-bases.

16. Vera Bergengruen, "Foursquare, Pokémon Go, And Now Fitbit—The US Military's Struggle With Popular Apps Is Not New," Buzzfeed.news, January 29, 2018, https://www.buzzfeednews.com/article/verabergeng ruen/foursquare-pokemon-go-and-now-fitbits-the-us-militarys.

17. Doug Laney, "3D Data Management: Controlling Data Volume, Velocity, and Variety," Meta Group report, February 6, 2001, https://study lib.net/doc/8647594/3d-data-management--controlling-data-volume --velocity--an... (accessed June 24, 2019).

18. John Gantz and David Reinsel, "Extracting Value from Chaos," in IDC iView (Sponsored by EMC Corporation), June 2011, 1–12.

19. Jennifer Dutcher, "What is Big Data?" datascience@Berkeley, Berkeley School of Information, September 3, 2014, available at https://gijn .org/2014/09/09/what-is-big-data/.

20. Gantz and Reinsel, "Extracting Value," 7.

Chapter 04. *Tiny Violence*

1. Jameel Jaffer, "Artist Trevor Paglen Talks to Jameel Jaffer About the Aesthetics of NSA Surveillance," ACLU, September 24, 2015, https:// www.aclu.org/blog/speak-freely/artist-trevor-paglen-talks-jameel-jaffer -about-aesthetics-nsa-surveillance.

2. Manoush Zomorodi and Alex Goldmark, "Eye in the Sky," *RadioLab*, podcast audio, June 18, 2015, http://www.radiolab.org/story/eye-sky/.

3. "Angel Fire," GlobalSecurity.org, http://www.globalsecurity.org/intell /systems/angel-fire.htm (accessed July 21, 2016).

4. Zomorodi and Goldmark, "Eye in the Sky."

5. Max Goncharov, "Russian Underground 101," Trend Micro Incorporated Research Paper, 2012, 12.

6. "Digital Attack Map," http://www.digitalattackmap.com (accessed December 2, 2015).

7. Igal Zeifman, "Q2 2015 Global DDoS Threat Landscape: Assaults Resemble Advanced Persistent Threats," Blog, Incapsula, July 9, 2015, https://www.incapsula.com/blog/ddos-global-threat-landscape-re port-q2-2015.html.

8. Emil Protalinski, "15-Year-Old Arrested for Hacking 259 Companies," ZDNet, April 17, 2012, http://www.zdnet.com/article/15-year-old -arrested-for-hacking-259-companies/.

9. Associated Press and MSNBC Staff, "Teen Held over Cyber Attacks Targeting US Government," Security on NBCnews.com, June 8, 2011, http://www.nbcnews.com/id/43322692/ns/technology_and_science -security/t/teen-held-over-cyber-attacks-targeting-us-government /#.VoqeOIRQh-P.

10. Mark Scott, "Teenager in Northern Ireland Is Arrested in TalkTalk Hacking Case," *New York Times*, October 27, 2015, http//www.nytimes .com/2015/10/28/technology/talktalk-hacking-arrest-northern-ireland .html?_r=0.

11. Chris Pollard, "The Boy Hackers: Teenagers Accessed the CIA, USAF, NHS, Sony, Nintendo…and the Sun," *Sun*, June 25, 2012, https:// www.thesun.co.uk/archives/news/712991/the-boy-hackers/.

12. Samuel Gibbs and Agencies, "Six Bailed Teenagers Accused of Cyber Attacks Using Lizard Squad Tool," *Guardian*, August 28, 2015, http:// www.theguardian.com/technology/2015/aug/28/teenagers-arrested -cyber-attacks-lizard-squad-stresser.

13. Kim Zetter, "Teen Who Hacked CIA Director's Email Tells How He Did It," *Wired*, October 19, 2015, http://www.wired.com/2015/10/hacker -who-broke-into-cia-director-john-brennan-email-tells-how-he-did-it/.

14. Nicole Perlroth, "Online Attacks on Infrastructure Are Increasing at a Worrying Pace," *Bits* (blog), *New York Times*, October 14, 2015, https:// bits.blogs.nytimes.com/2015/10/14/online-attacks-on-infrastructure -are-increasing-at-a-worrying-pace/.

15. Perlroth, "Online Attacks."

16. John Arquilla and David Ronfeldt, "The Advent of Netwar (Revisited)," in John Arquilla and David Ronfeldt, eds., *Networks and Netwars: The Future of Terror, Crime, and Militancy* (Santa Monica, CA: Rand Corporation, 2001), 6–7.

17. I am grateful to Soyoung Yoon for bringing the Obadikes' work to my attention and for her penetrating essay about their work, "Do a Number: The Facticity of the Voice, or Reading Stop-and-Frisk Data," *Discourse: Journal for Theoretical Studies in Media and Culture* 39, no. 3 (2017).

18. Mendi and Keith Obadike, "Numbers Station 1 [Furtive Movements]— Excerpt," filmed at the Ryan Lee Gallery, 2015, video, 2:47, YouTube, https://www.youtube.com/watch?v=PuLzv53gM_o (accessed November 14, 2018).

Chapter 05. *The Numb of Numbers*

1. "Long and Short Scales," Wikipedia, https://en.wikipedia.org/wiki /Long_and_short_scales (accessed November 10, 2015).

2. In November 2014, technology writer and cofounder of *Wired* magazine Kevin Kelly posted the following message on Twitter: "No wonder

I am confused. A billion is not a billion, a quadrillion not a quadrillion. Depends on where you live. Fix?" Twitter, November 20, 2014, https://twitter.com/kevin2kelly/status/535526708552945664.

3. "Long and Short Scales."

4. "Indian Numbering System," Wikipedia, https://en.wikipedia.org/wiki/Indian_numbering_system (accessed November 10, 2015).

5. Tom Geoghegan, "Is Trillion the New Billion?" *BBC News Magazine*, October 28, 2011, http://www.bbc.com/news/magazine-15478580.

6. David McCandless has visualized those things that we now count in trillions of dollars at his remarkable website, Information Is Beautiful. "$Trillions," Information Is Beautiful, https://informationisbeautiful.net/visualizations/trillions-what-is-a-trillion-dollars/.

7. Geoghegan, "Is Trillion the New Billion?"

8. Two important keys for a rise in affect are images and attention. As Paul Slovic writes in "Psychic Numbing and Genocide," "Underlying the role of affect in the experiential system is the importance of images, to which positive or negative feelings become attached. Images in this system include not only visual images, important as these may be, but words, sounds, smells, memories, and products of our imagination." Paul Slovic, "Psychic Numbing and Genocide," American Psychological Association, November 2007, http://www.apa.org/science/about/2007/11/slovic.aspx.

9. Mass shooting data from "Past Summary Ledgers," Gun Violence Archive, https://www.gunviolencearchive.org/past-tolls (accessed May 4, 2019); election spending in the U.S. from "The Cost of Election," OpenSecrets.org, https://www.opensecrets.org/overview/cost.php (accessed May 4, 2019).

10. David McCandless, "The Billion Dollar-o-Gram 2013," Information Is Beautiful, http://informationisbeautiful.net/visualizations/billion-dollar-o-gram-2013/ (accessed December 9, 2015).

11. I am indebted to my colleague Dr. Mindy Fullilove for bringing this frame of "400 years of inequality" to my attention. Her initiative can be found here: http://www.400yearsofinequality.org.

12. Tatiana Schlossberg, "Japan Is Obsessed with Climate Change. Young People Don't Get It," *New York Times*, December 5, 2016, https://www.nytimes.com/2016/12/05/science/japan-global-warming.html.

13. Hendrik Hertzberg, *One Million* (New York: Abrams, 2009), x.

Chapter 06. *Scalar Framing*

1. Astronaut photograph AS17-148-22727 courtesy NASA Johnson Space Center Gateway to Astronaut Photography of Earth, https://eol.jsc.nasa .gov/SearchPhotos/photo.pl?mission=AS17&roll=148&frame=22727.

2. Kees Boeke, *Cosmic View: The Universe in 40 Jumps* (New York: John Day, 1957).

3. Within the powers of ten, however, a subtle categorical shift in kind happens along the sliding scale, as social units (individual, family, community) become geographical units (the city, the region, the country, etc.). This happens, in part, because we have difficulty conceiving of social units that span the population of a city.

4. In his book *The Botany of Desire: A Plant's-Eye View of the World* (New York: Random House, 2001), Michael Pollan demonstrates the ways in which four specific cultivars (apples, tulips, marijuana, potatoes) take advantage of human tendencies to advance their own genetic agenda, letting us know that we ignore their capacity for agency at the risk of our own myopia and environmental peril.

5. "Bicycle Production Reaches 130 Million Units," Worldwatch Institute, http://www.worldwatch.org/node/5462 (accessed February 3, 2016). They get their figures from "World Players in the Bicycle Market," in John Crenshaw, "China's Two-Wheeled Juggernaut Keeps Rolling Along," *Bicycle Retailer and Industry News*, (April 1, 2006), 40.

6. The imagery that follows for this example draws upon Google Maps' satellite imagery of New York City. Map data copyright © Google, Maxar Technologies.

7. Donella Meadows, *Thinking in Systems* (White River Junction, VT: Chelsea Green Publishing, 2008), 108.

Chapter 07. *The Middle*

1. Cade Metz, "Google Is 2 Billion Lines of Code—and It's All in One Place," *Wired*, September 16, 2015, http://www.wired.com/2015/09 /google-2-billion-lines-codeand-one-place/.

2. "Linux Kernel Development: Version 4.13," The Linux Foundation, https://www.linuxfoundation.org/2017-linux-kernel-report-landing -page/ (accessed on March 30, 2019).

3. Linus Torvalds, quoted in Steven Weber, *The Success of Open Source* (Cambridge MA: Harvard University Press, 2004), 55.

4. Weber, *Open Source*, 67.
5. Linus Torvalds, quoted in Weber, *Open Source,* 90.
6. "Usage Share of Operating Systems," Wikipedia, last modified December, 19, 2018, https://en.wikipedia.org/wiki/Usage_share_of_operating_systems (accessed December, 21, 2018).
7. Quentin Hardy, "Microsoft Opens Its Corporate Data Software to Linux," *New York Times*, March 7, 2016, https://www.nytimes.com/2016/03/08/technology/microsoft-opens-its-corporate-data-software-to-linux.html.
8. In September 2018 the *New Yorker* reported that Linus Torvalds was stepping aside from his role of "benevolent dictator" over the Linux source code to address his caustic and abusive comments toward others in his management of the software development process. Noam Cohen, "After Years of Abusive E-mails, the Creator of Linux Steps Aside," *New Yorker*, September 19, 2018, https://www.newyorker.com/science/elements/after-years-of-abusive-e-mails-the-creator-of-linux-steps-aside.

Chapter 08. *Feral Pigs and Wicked Problems*

1. Paul Ehrlich and Anne Ehrlich, *The Population Explosion* (New York: Simon & Schuster, 1990), 36–37.
2. John Morthland, "A Plague of Pigs in Texas," Smithsonian.com, January 2011, http://www.smithsonianmag.com/science-nature/a-plague-of-pigs-in-texas-73769069/#Mj1QzdFSOEhxZDVu.99.
3. Kyle Settle, "Virginia Feral Hog Population Becoming a Major Nuisance," Wide Open Spaces, October 2, 2014, http://www.wideopenspaces.com/feral-hog-population-exploding-virginia/.
4. Morthland, "Plague of Pigs."
5. Horst Rittel and Melvin Webber, "Dilemmas in a General Theory of Planning," *Policy Sciences* 4 (1973), 169.
6. Christopher C. M. Kyba et al., "Artificially Lit Surface of Earth at Night Increasing in Radiance and Extent," Science Advances, November 22, 2017, https://advances.sciencemag.org/content/3/11/e1701528.
7. Donella Meadows, *Thinking in Systems* (White River Junction, VT: Chelsea Green Publishing, 2008), 168–9.
8. Meadows, *Systems*, 170.
9. Meadows doubles down on design—"Systems can't be controlled, but they can be designed and redesigned" (Meadows, *Systems*, 169). Rittel

and Webber reach a similar conclusion as well, "Social problems are never solved. At best they are only re-solved—over and over again" (Rittel and Webber, "Dilemmas," 160).

10. Tom Vanderbilt, "The Traffic Guru," *Wilson Quarterly*, Summer 2008, http://archive.wilsonquarterly.com/essays/traffic-guru.

11. Vanderbilt, "Traffic Guru."

12. I am grateful to my nephew, Andrew Verville, for this observation about the number of street signs.

13. Vanderbilt, "Traffic Guru."

Chapter 09. *Presence*

1. George E. P. Box, J. Stuart Hunter, and William G. Hunter, *Statistics for Experimenters: Design, Innovation and Discovery*, 2nd ed. (Hoboken, NJ: Wiley Interscience, 2005), 440.

2. Jorge Luis Borges, "On Exactitude in Science" in *The Aleph and Other Stories*, trans. Andrew Hurley (New York: Penguin, 2000), 181.

3. Casey N. Cep, "The Allure of the Map," *New Yorker*, January 22, 2014.

4. Bill Gaver, "SonicFinder," uploaded 2016, video, 2:44, Vimeo, https://vimeo.com/channels/billgaver/158610127. Thanks to Shannon Mattern for this reference.

5. Mark Wilson, "75% of Ikea's Catalog Is Computer Generated Imagery: You Could Have Fooled Us. Wait, Actually, You Did," *Fast Company*, August 29, 2014, https://www.fastcompany.com/3034975/75-of-ikeas-catalog-is-computer-generated-imagery.

6. Jonathan Foote, "Ethos Pathos Logos: Architects and Their Chairs," in *Scale: Imagination, Perception, and Practice in Architecture*, eds. Gerald Adler, Timothy Brittain-Catlin, and Gordana Fontana-Giusti (New York: Routledge, 2012), 160.

Index

Page numbers of illustrations appear in italics.

Adams, John Quincy, 30, 35–36
Afghanistan War, 67–69
    "Afghanistan Stability: COIN
        Dynamics" diagram, 67–68,
        68, 69
    secret U.S. base revealed by Strava's
        data, 89
AI (artificial intelligence), 98–99, 100
Airbnb, 204
alienation, 46–47
    capitalism and, 47
    industrial age, urbanization, and,
        47–48
    the unconscious and, 47, 93
Al-Khalili, Jim, 75
Amazon, 86, 99
    retail distribution centers, 135
Amazon Web Services, 86–87
American Civil Liberties Union
    (ACLU)
    stop-and-frisk policing and, 121–22
    surveillance and civil liberty
        concerns, 103, 109
ampere, 31
Anderson, Chris, 80–81, 240n13
    Free: How Today's Smartest Businesses
        Profit by Giving Something for
        Nothing, 81, 82, 84–86
ant behavior, scale and, 71–72
Apple, 159
    data amassed, 99
    SonicFinder and, 228

Apple App Store, 2–3
Apple Maps, 89
aproportionality, 80, 104–5
Arbor Networks, 112, *113*
Arquilla, John
    The Future of Terror, Crime, and
        Militancy, 118
    netwar and, 118–19
asymmetry. *See* scalar asymmetry
attunement, 184–85, 196, 214, 215,
    231, 232

banks, banking industry, 14
    hackers and, 15–16
    mortgage-backed security, 15
    mortgages and, 14–15
Bartholl, Aram
    Map, *17*, 17–18
Baudelaire, Charles, 47
behavior
    data on, tracking, 88–89, 93, 95,
        96, 121
    email and, 8
    physical laws and scale, 72
    quantum level, 75
    scale and, 9, 19, 20, 70–72, 188
    Monderman's traffic engineering and,
        216–20, *217*, *219*
    system behavior, 19, 72, 74, 162, 179,
        180, 204, 211, 213
Benjamin, Walter, 47
Bernstein, Elmer, 142, 143

bicycling
    advantages of, 157
    bike lanes and, 154
    bike-share systems, 153, 155–56, 203
    environmental impact of, 160–61
    federal government and, 158–59
    global urban bicycle riding rates, 150
    most cycled cities, 150
    scalar framing, New York City and,
        149–61
big data. *See* data and big data
"Big Data Is Not the Created Content
        nor Is It Even Its Consumption—It
        Is the Analysis of All of the Data
        Surrounding or Swirling Around
        It" (IDC), 97
BIPM (International Bureau of Weights
        and Measures), 28, 31
    kilogram and, 34–35, 238n8
    meter defined by, 35
    second defined by, 41–42
    seven basic standard units of, 31, 35
    time measurement decoupled from
        Earth's rotation, 42
Blacktop (film), 142
Blind Justice, 36
Boeke, Kees
    *Cosmic View: The Universe in 40
        Jumps*, 143
Borges, Jorge Luis, 21–22
    "On Exactitude in Science," 225–26
*Botany of Desire, The: A Plant's-Eye View
        of the World* (Pollan), 244n4
Box, George, 223
broken systems, 12–13, 136, 211
Brooks, David, 12–13
bubble level, as instrument of spatial
        orientation, 1–5
Bumiller, Elisabeth, 67–69
Bush, George W., 106
butterfly metamorphosis, 72–74
    imaginal discs and, 73
    persistence of memory and, 73–74

calendars, and marking orientation in
        linear time, 5
candela, 31
Cep, Casey, 226
CERN, Large Hadron Collider, 39
CGPM (General Conference on
        Weights and Measures), 31
Chaplin, Charlie, 48
Chinese measurement systems, 33
church organ, 45
Citi Bike, 153, 155
climate change, 12
    decision-making and, 165–66
    environmentalist's mantra, 201
    global ecosystems and, 211
    Japanese government strategy,
        134–35
    nonhuman points of view and, 149,
        244n4
    "Paper or plastic?" query, 9–10, 166,
        201
    problem-solving and, 173
    reconnecting to human scale, 134–36
    recycling plastic bottles, unexpected
        consequences, 165
    Running the Numbers (Jordan)
        depiction of, 130–31, *131*
    scalar framing and, 149, 160–61
clocks, and marking orientation in
        linear time, 1, 2, 5
    See also time
coastline paradox, 40–41
communication, 139
    in bottom-up systems, 178, 179
    digital, 7–8, 16
    feedback, 97, 179, 183, 185–86,
        187–88, 189, 190–91, 192, 197,
        198–99, 203, 214, 215, 221, 231
    numbers stations, 120
    packet switching, email, and, 7
    presence and, 231
    scaffolding and, 187–88, 198–99,
        203, 221

surveillance of, 103
in top-down systems, 176
compass, as instrument of spatial
    orientation, 1, 2, 5
complexity, complex systems, 4, 70, 76,
    205–12, 221–22, 231
  embracing, 20
  networked world and, 15
  powers of ten and, 148
  problem-solving, scaffolding, and,
    192, 194, 199, 201, 205–15,
    221–22, 245–46n9
  scalar framing for dealing with,
    149, 158
computers
  dematerialization of the knowable
    and, 3
  early input devices, punch cards, 228
  entanglement and, 14–16
  files on, 6
  hackers, 15–16, 112, 115–16, 117,
    178, 191–92, 196
  Linux operating system, 189–99
  Moore's law, 81
  operating systems for, 189–90
  physical matter replaced by, 6,
    13–14, 16
  scale removed from, 228
  shrinking size of, 6
  storage of, 6, 8
  structured data on, 93–94
  term for the human body as
    "meat," 230
  visual metaphors of files, desktops,
    trash cans, 228–29
  See also digital world
Concord, N.H., 52
  traffic circle, 220, *221*
Conway, Drew, 92
Cosmic View: The Universe in 40 Jumps
    (Boeke), 143
Crease, Robert
  The World in the Balance, 32

dark web, 16
DARPA (U.S. Defense Advanced
    Research Projects Agency), 110
data analytics, 93, 94
data and big data, 67–70, 86–100, 231
  AI and, 98–99
  Amazon Web Services and, 86–87
  big data definitions, 90, 91–93
  "Big Data Is Not the Created Content
    nor Is It Even Its Consumption—It
    Is the Analysis of All of the Data
    Surrounding or Swirling Around
    It" (IDC), 97
  cognitive overload and, 69
  companies with most amassed data, 99
  data privacy and, 88–90
  Excel spreadsheets and, 90
  fitness tracking bands, unintended
    consequences of, 88–90
  inflicting harm and, 120
  metadata, 96
  metadata becoming metaphysics, 93
  mining big data, promise of discovery
    and, 93, 98
  movement of facts to meaning, 98
  Netflix and, 87–88
  "phase change" and, 86, 93, 98, 99
  quantifying experience and, 120, 231
  quantity altering quality of, 67–69, *68*
  Strava global heatmap, 88–89
  structured data, 93–94, 95, 96–97
  "3V" framework, 90
  Uber as a big data company, 97, 99,
    100
  unstructured data, 94, 95–96
  value as mysterious supplement from
    bigness, 90–91, 93
DDoS (distributed denial of service)
    attack, 111–15
  Google's Digital Attack Map and,
    112–13, *113*, 117
  Imperva Incapsula key findings
    about, 114

DeBergi, Marty, 23–24, 25
decision-making
    certainty and scale of impact,
        169–70
    scaffolding for, 184–200
    scalar framing for, 165–67
    top-down systems and, 175–76
    See also problem-solving
Different Kind of Order, A (art exhibit),
    101
digital economy, 80–86
digital world, 7, 16–17, 232
    business and, 14, 80–86, 135
    communities uncoupled from
        geography in, 148–49
    digital images, perceptual gap
        between on-screen and real life, *79*,
        79–80, 224–25
    immateriality and, 3, 6, 13–14, 16,
        80, 136
    immersion in digital spaces, 223–24
    Microsoft Word and perceptual gap,
        77–78, 80, 224
    perceptual cues distorted by, 80,
        224
    "presence" needed in, 228, 230–32
    replacing physical world, 6, 13–14, 16
    scalar framing for, 148–49
    scale removed from, 228
    surveillance and, 101–9
    unstructured data and, 94–95
    visual metaphors of files, desktops,
        trash cans, 228–29
"Dilemmas in a General Theory of
    Planning" (Rittel and Webber),
    208, 210–11
Drachten, Netherlands, 216–20, *217*,
    219
Dutcher, Jennifer, 91

Eames, Charles and Ray, 171, 172, 213
    Blacktop, 142
    originality of vision, 141

Powers of Ten, 141, 142–48, *144*, *145*
    Toccata for Toy Trains, 142
economy, business
    digital marketplace and value, 80–86
    "free" goods and services, 81–85, 196,
        240n13
    Google market strategy, 82
    Radiohead's direct sales, 82–83
    reconnecting to human scale, 135
    scaling up and, 203–4
    Wikipedia, 83–84
education
    improving public schools, 10–11
    public school system, disarray of, 12
    scalar framing for approaching
        problems in, 167–70
    Zuckerberg, Newark, and, 12, 167,
        211
Ehrlich, Anne and Paul
    The Population Explosion, 201–2
Einstein, Albert, 75
email, 7–8
    "Is Email Making Professors
        Stupid?," 8
    packet switching and, 7
    shift in scale, consequences of, 8
    social behaviors and, 8
entanglement, 13, 14–16, 148, 222,
    224, 228, 232
    digital images, perceptual gap
        between on-screen and real life, *79*,
        79–80, 224–25
    infrastructure of
        interconnectedness, 16
    Microsoft Word and perceptual gap,
        77–78
    our relationship to scale as, 77
    perceptional universe and, 77–80
    in quantum physics, 76–77
environments, human interaction with
    circus and the fairground, 54
    digitally mediated, 3–4, 18, 66
    figure/ground relationships, 45–66

four cities compared, 50–63, *51*, *53*
industrial age and urbanization,
    46–48, 65
scale and spectacle, impact of, 45–46
scale as orienting ourselves to, 4
traditional, geographically bound, 3
Vantablack and, 62–65, *63*

Facebook, 12, 99, 221
facial recognition software, 98
Family Romance sculpture (Ray),
    54–55, *55*
figure/ground relationships, 45–66
    in art, 54–55, *55*
    "The Blue Marble" and, *140*, 140–41
    changes of size as experiential, 54
    in children's books, 54
    Concord, N.H., 52
    corporeal relations to scale, 49, 54
    defined, 56, 57
    Greensboro, Vt., 52, *53*
    industrial age, urbanization, and
        alienation, 46–48, 65
    information age (digital world) and,
        65–66
    lightning and sky, *56*
    New York City and, 50, *51*, 51–52, 53
    perception of, shifting over a lifetime,
        55–56
    Philadelphia and, 51
    photographic images and, 58–62, *59*,
        60, *62*
    relationships between the human
        body, human perception, human
        agency, and scale, 53
    relevance of, 230
    scale and establishing a platform of
        predictability, 49
    solitary figure against the ground of
        stairs and sky, 57, *57*
    Vantablack and, 62–65, 66
Fincher, David, 87–88
fitness tracking bands, 88

Forbes magazine, 202
Foucault, Michel
    The Order of Things, 21–22
*Free: How Today's Smartest Businesses
    Profit by Giving Something for
    Nothing* (Anderson), 81, 82, 84–86
    free digital versions of, 85–86
Freud, Sigmund, 47, 93
Friedman, Tom, 54
Fullilove, Mindy, 243n11
*Future of Terror, Crime, and Militancy,
    The* (Arquilla and Ronfeldt),
    118–19
Futurism, 48

Gaver, Bill, 228
gigabyte, 6
GMT (Greenwich Mean Time), 42
Google, 99
    Ad Sense, 83
    code base, lines of code in, 190
    Digital Attack Map, 112–13, *113*,
        117
    digital economy and, 82
    information flow and, 110
Google Books, 85
Google Maps, 17, 89, 147, 244n6
gravity
    Earth's shape and, 37, 38
    "The Gnome Experiment" (exploring
        variations in gravity), 36–39, *37*
    human scale and classical
        (Newtonian) mechanics, 72
    at Nanyuki, Kenya vs. South Pole, 38
Greensboro, Vt., 52, *53*

hackers, 15–16, 112, 115–16, 117
    IKEA hackers and website, 178
    Linux and, 191–92, 196
Hayden, Michael V., 118
Hertzberg, Hendrik
    One Million, *136*, 136–37
holometabolous organisms, 74

House of Cards (Netflix series), 87–88
HPLC (high-performance liquid
    chromatography), 27

IBUs (international bitterness units),
    26–27
isohumulone measured by, 27
IDC company, 90
    report on big data (2011), 97
IKEA, 22
    hackers and hacker website, 178
    product images as digital
        constructions, 229
    immateriality, 3, 6, 13–14, 16, 80,
        136, 204
    as digital dematerialization of our
        artifacts, processes, and services, 16
imperial system of measure, 32–33
    "foot" and, 33
    word *ruler* and, 33
    "yard," 35
Imperva Incapsula, 114
    "Q2 2015 Global DDoS Threat
        Landscape: Assaults Resemble
        Advanced Persistent Threats," 114
Industrial Age, 46–48, 174
Information Is Beautiful website, 128,
    243n6
infrastructure. *See* scaffolding
internet
    cybercrime, 112–16
    DDoS cyberattack, 111–15
    growth of, 111
    information flow and, 110
    "netwar," 117–19
    ransomware, 115
    vulnerability of, cyberattacks and, 111
    See also digital world
Iraq War, 106
    Falluja, surveillance of, 106–7, 108
    IEDs and "Project Angelfire," 106–7
"Is Email Making Professors Stupid?"
    (*Chronicle Review*), 8

"Is Trillion the New Billion?" (*BBC
    News Magazine*), 125
ITU (International Telecommunication
    Union), 42

Jaffer, Jameel, 103
Jaquith, Waldo, 240n13
Jordan, Chris
    Running the Numbers, 130–31, *131*
Juarez, Mexico, 108

Kapoor, Anish, 64
Kelly, Kevin, 242–43n2
kelvin, 31
Kern, 36
    "The Gnome Experiment" (exploring
        variations in gravity), 36–39, 42
    Gnome Kit, *37*
    model EWB 2.4 scale, 36
kilogram, 31, 33
    determining the standard weight of,
        27–29, 34–35
    loss of mass, 27–28, 36
    platinum artifact for fixed standards
        of, 28, 34, 238n8
    revised definition of, 238n8
    SI definition of, 32, 33
    variations in gravity and weight of,
        38–39
Koons, Jeff, 54

Laney, Doug, 90
Leonardo da Vinci
    "The Vitruvian Man," 35
Li, Tongcang, 76
Linux operating system, 189–99
    bottom-up production process, 193,
        199
    collaborative infrastructure for,
        190–92
    consumer-producer distinction
        blurred, 194–95, 198
    free flow of information and, 198–99

innovative licensing scheme (GNU), 193, 197
launching of, 190, 191–92
lines of code in, 191
"Linus doesn't scale" problem, 194
Linux 1.0 release, 192
"pipes" and "ports" mechanism for, 198
products using, 195
scaffolded models, 196–99
success of, 195
three key strategies (or rules) for collaborative source code, 192–93
top-down administration of, 193, 194, 197, 199, 245n8
Torvalds opening post of 1991 explaining the program, 191–92
Torvalds post of 1992 on control of content, 193–94
liter, 33
Lyall, Sarah, 27–28, 36

management sciences, 48, 174
Map (Bartholl), *17*, 17–18
maps, 5, 225–26, 227
Martin, Agnes
  The Tree, 57, *57*
Marx, Karl, 47
McCandless, David, 230, 243n6
  "The Billion Dollar-o-Gram," *128*, 128–30
McChrystal, Stanley, 67–69, 227
McFadden, Johnjoe, 75
McNutt, Ross, 106, 107, 108, 109
Meadows, Donella, 19, 163–64, 211–12, 214, 245–46n9
measurement, 19, 23–44, 238n16
  coastline paradox, 40–41
  decoupling from experience, 134, 227
  fairness, justice, and equality and, 36
  first universalizing, fixed standards for, 33–34
  first U.S. law on standards for, 29–30

human body and perception
  decentered from, 35, 36, 43–44, 126
  IBUs (for beer), 26–27
  metric system and, 29–30, 33
  peculiarities and irregularities of, 39
  political issues, 32
  quantifying the qualitative, 40, 43
  quantitative scales and, 26–27
  scale as, 26
  search for precise and accurate, 26, 29, 36, 44
  SHUs for hot peppers, 27
  systems based on the body, 33, 34, 35
  technical quest to define units of, 32
  of time, variability and, 41–43
  universal standards for, 28–36
  of weight, and variations in gravity, 38–39
metaphysical naturalism, 25
meter, 31, 33–34
  BIPM definition, 35
metric system, 29–30
  countries adopting, 33
  platinum artifacts for fixed standards of, 28, 33, 34, 238n8
  SI and, 33
Microsoft, 99
  SQL Server on Linux, 195
Microsoft Windows 10, 189–90
  computer code in, 189
Microsoft Word, 189
  on-screen images and the perception of scale, 77–78, 80, 224
Minix, 190, 191, 196
models, scale models, 142, 223, 226–27
  architectural, 18
  business models, 18, 99
Modern Times (film), 48
mole (amount of substance), 31
Monderman, Hans, 216–21, *217, 219, 221*, 222, 230
Moore's law, 81

Morrison, Philip and Phylis, 143, 144, 146
Moses, Robert, 210
Mulligan, Deirdre, 92

Nanduri, Prakash, 91–92
Nanyuki, Kenya, 38
Negroponte, Nicholas, 13
Netflix, 87–88
    House of Cards, 87–88
Netherlands Fallacy, 201–2
netwar, 106, 118–19
networks, networked, 3, 15, 19–20, 81,
        86, 98, 105, 110–11, 149, 179, 184,
        211, 227–28, 230, 231, 232
    as infrastructure, 14, 16
    netwar and hackers, 115, 116, 117,
        118–19
    Strava's global, of athletes, 89–90
    surveillance and, 102, 103
    wicked problems and, 201
Newark, N.J.
    using scalar framing to improve the
        school system, 167–70
    Zuckerberg and the public school
        system, 12, 167, 211
Newton, Isaac, 72, 76
Newtonian (classical) physics, 72
New York, New York, 50, *51*, 51–52, 53,
        244n6
    bicycling in, scalar framing and,
        149–61, *151*, *153*, *155*, *156*, *158*, *160*
    bike-share systems (Citi Bike), 153,
        155–56
    Cross Bronx Expressway and, 210
    mass transit in, 150
    regional commuters, transit systems,
        157–58
    stop-and-frisk policing strategy,
        121–22
New York Times
    article on cyberattacks, 117–18
    Bumiller article on military briefing,
        Afghanistan, 67–69, *68*

Lyall's article on the kilogram,
        27–28, 36
numbers, 123–37
    big numbers decoupled from human
        experience (numbing effect),
        126–27, 243n8, 243n11
    billion, defining what it is, 123–24,
        125, 242–43n2
    Chinese systems, 124
    Hertzberg's book *One Million*, *136*,
        136–37
    home purchase, 130
    Indian (or Vedic) system, 124
    Jordan's *Running the Numbers*,
        130–31, *131*
    long scale vs. short scale system,
        123–25, *125*
    McCandless's "The Billion
        Dollar-o-Gram," *128*, 128–30
    quadrillion, 125, 242–43n2
    systems, varying types globally, 124
    translation and materialization to
        connect with the unthinkably
        large, 127–37, *128*, *131*, *133*, *136*
    trillion, 123, 124, 125, 243n6
    Walker's *A Subtlety, or the Marvelous
        Sugar Baby*, 132–34, *133*
number station, 120–21
Numbers Station [Furtive Movements]
        (Obadike), 120–21, *121*, 122

Obadike, Keith and Mendi, 230,
        242n17
    Numbers Station [Furtive Movements],
        120–21, *121*, 122
Ogilvy & Mather advertising agency, 37
Oldenburg, Claes, 54
One Million (Hertzberg), *136*, 136–37
"On Exactitude in Science" (Borges),
        225–26
Order of Things, The (Foucault),
        21–22
O'Reilly, Tim, 85

packet switching, 7
Paglen, Trevor, 102–3, 106, 109
    Untitled (Reaper Drone), 101–2, *102*,
        103
"Paper or plastic?" query, 9–10, 166,
    201
Participatory Budgeting movement, 222
Pauling, Linus, 185
phase change (from experience to
        information)
    AI and surveillance systems, 98
    big data and, 86, 90, 91
    butterfly metamorphosis as, 73
    home buying, scale of numbers and,
        130
    quantitative shifts become qualitative
        transformations, 93
    tiny violence and, 122
Philadelphia, Pa.
    human scale of, 51
    New York vs., 51–52
Philosophical Investigations
    (Wittgenstein), 28–29
photographs, 58–62, 229–30
    "The Blue Marble," 139–41, *140*
    data on images uploaded to a social
        media site, 96–97
    digital, as unstructured data, 94–96
    *A fishing boat (figure) emerges from the
        fog (ground)*, 59–60, *60*, 61
    manipulation of scale in, 58–59, 60
    Paglen's, 102–3, 106, 109
    perception of size and, 58–59, 61–62,
        62, *79*, 79–80, 100, 224–25
    statue of Saddam Hussein, image
        frame and, 60–61
    unstable figure/ground relationship,
        59, *59*
    Untitled (Reaper Drone), 101–2, *102*,
        103
    using the human figure for scale on
        Amazon.com, 61, *62*
    as visual scale model, 61–62, 226

physical world, 16–17
    replaced by digital world, 6, 13–14, 16
policing, scalar shifts and, 121–22,
    202–3
Pollan, Michael
    *Botany of Desire, The: A Plant's-Eye
        View of the World*, 244n4
Population Explosion, The (Ehrlich),
    201–2
Powers of Ten (film), 141, 142–48, *144*,
    145, 170, 171, 172
PPS (Persistent Surveillance Systems),
    107
    technology, advances in, 108–9
    use in Juarez, Mexico, 108
    presence, 223–32
    in digital environments, 223–24.
        227–29
    representation, reality, and scale,
        224–27
    thinking through scale and, 229–32
problem-solving, scalar influences on,
    201–21
    bottom-up (self-organizing or
        emergent) approaches, 177–80,
        181, 188, 191, 193, 199
    change agents and, 201
    complexity and, 205–15, 221–22,
        245–46n9
    do-it-yourself (DIY) movement, 178
    enlisting stakeholders in, 173–74,
        190–92, 221
    example, bicycling in New York City,
        149–61
    example, how to improve the Newark,
        N.J., school system, 167–70
    example, shift from incandescent to
        LED lightbulbs, 211
    example, wild pigs in the rural
        Southwest, 206–7
    just solutions for, 209–10
    Monderman's traffic problem,
        216–21, *217*, *219*, *221*

problem-solving, scalar influences on
(*cont.*)
  Netherlands Fallacy, 201–2
  scaffolding and, 174, 180–200, *183*
  scaffolding and Linux operating
    system, 189–99
  scalar framing and, 149–70
  scaling from the middle and, 178–200
  scaling model of innovation and, 205–6
  scaling theory of change and, 202–3
  of small-scale problems, 173
  top-down approaches, 174–77, 180,
    181, 188, 191, 193, 197, 199
  wicked problems and, 208–9, 211, 214
  Zeno's paradox and, 215
"Psychic Numbing and Genocide"
    (Slovic), 243n8
publishing
  internet and digital publishing, 85–86
  O'Reilly's adage, 85
  "Q2 2015 Global DDoS Threat
    Landscape: Assaults Resemble
    Advanced Persistent Threats"
    (Imperva Incapsula), 114

qualitative measurement, 26, 40
  bitterness of beer and, 26–17
  hot pepper heat and, 27
quantum level, quantum mechanics,
    75–77
  Einstein on, 75
  entanglement and, 76–77
  quantum biology, 75–76
  scale and, 75–76
  superposition, 75–77, 100

Radiohead, 82–83
  In Rainbows album, 83
Rand Corporation
  *The Future of Terror, Crime, and
    Militancy*, 117–19
Ray, Charles, 54
  Family Romance sculpture, 54–55, *55*

reality
  computer-generated simulations vs.,
    229
  digital images, perceptual gap
    between on-screen and real life, *79*,
    79–80, 224–25, 227
  maps and, 225–26, 227
  representations of, 224–26
  scale models of, 18, 226–27
  signifiers and, 227
  virtual, augmented, and mixed
    realities, 18, 65–66, 229
  See also digital world
Richardson, Lewis Fry, 39–40
Rittel, Horst, 245–46n9
  "Dilemmas in a General Theory of
    Planning," 208, 210–11
Ronfeldt, David
  *The Future of Terror, Crime, and
    Militancy*, 118
  netwar and, 118–19
Running the Numbers (Jordan), 130–31,
    131

Sauter, Albert, 37
scaffolding, 20, 174, 180–200, *183*
  attunement step for, 184–85, 196
  for complex systems, 215–16, 221–22
  consumption and, 187–88
  example, Linux operating system,
    189–99
  example, rose lattice, 182, 186
  feedback step for, 187–88, 198–99,
    203, 221
  forms of, 182–83
  how to start, 184
  ideation step for, 185, 196–97
  lessons to guide the process, 188–89
  paradox of, 199–200
  programming step for, 186, 197–98
  prototyping step for, 185–86, 197
  recursion step for, 186–87, 198
  what it is, 182–83

scalar aptitudes of young children,
54, 55
scalar asymmetry
change and, 202
defined, 72
cyberattacks and, 116–17, 118
warfare, violence, and, 80, 105, 109,
110, 112
scalar ethics, 166
scalar framing, 20, 139–72, 213
anthropocentric (human point of
view), 149, 244n4
bias, individual points of view and,
170–72
"The Blue Marble" and, 139–41, *140*
decision-making and, 165–67
efficacy of, 149–51, 165
example, bicycling in New York City,
149–61
example, changing the Newark
school-system, 167–70
example, Monderman's traffic
engineering and, 218
four lessons of, 162–64
Google Maps and, 147
Powers of Ten and, 141, 142–48, 170,
171, 172
powers of ten as a frame, 148, 149–61,
151, *153*, *155*, *156*, *158*, *160*, *161*,
167–70, 218, 244n3
problem-solving and, 167–70
trap of, 170–71
visual system transformed from
earthbound to cosmic, 139–47
what it does, 147–48, 164–65
what it is, 148
scalar shifts
in butterfly metamorphosis, 72–74,
162
capabilities of an organism and size,
71–72
of data, 67–69, *68*, 86–100
digital economy and, 80–86

nature of reality and, 74
quantum level behaviors and, 75–77
scalar framing and, 162
scalar variance or scalar asymmetry,
72 (*see also* scalar asymmetry)
on-screen images and the perception
of scale, 77–80, *79*, 224–25
system behaviors and, 69–70, 72, 74
scalar variance, 72
scale
abstractions of, strategies for
providing sensory cues, 127, *128*,
128–37, *131*, *133*, *136*, 228
behavior and, 70–72, 166, 167–70
big numbers and, 123–37
data and big data, 67–69, *68*, 86–100
decision-making using, 165–67,
169–70
decoupling from human experience,
3, 4, 134, 227
definition of, 4
digital forms of, 4, 7
digital surveillance and, 101–9
emotional impact of scale changes,
45, 46, 54, 65
entanglement and the perception of
scale, 13, 14–16, 77–80, 148, 224
figure/ground relationships and,
45–66
global thinking and, 11–12, 160–61
how we learn about scale, 49–50
human body and perception of, 33,
229–30
information and, 110–11
instrumentation of, 5
measurement and, 5, 19, 23–44,
238n16
the middle and scaling ideas, 180–82
perceptual and conceptual scale, 46,
103, 105, 188
presence and, 223–32
photographic images and, 58–62, *59*,
60, *62*, 100, 224

scale (*cont.*)
  physical effects of, 46
  problem-solving and, 201–21
  proliferation, small ideas scaling and,
    186
  psychological effects of, 46–48
  quantum level, 75–77
  reality and, 65, 74, *79*, 79–80, 127,
    224–27
  scaffolding and, 174, 180–200, *183*
  scalar framing, 139–72
  scalar shifts, 4, 8, 9, 10, 67–100
  on-screen images and the perception
    of scale, 77–80, *79*
  thinking and acting through, 4,
    18–19, 229–30
  tiny violence, *102*, 109–22, *113*, *121*
  what it is, 4, 224
scaling theory of change, 202–3
scaling up, 203
Scribd, 85
Sèvres, France, 28
  kilogram prototype in, 28
  kilogram weight in, location and, 38
SHUs (Scoville Heat units), 27
  HPLC and capsaicin measurement, 27
SI (International System of Units), 31
  metric system and, 33
Simmons, Laurie, 54
"Size of Man, The" (Went), 70
Slovic, Paul
  "Psychic Numbing and Genocide,"
    243n8
smart phone
  apps available for, number of, 2–3
  multifunctions of, 2
  tools as functions on (utilities), 1, 2, 5
social media
  communities uncoupled from
    geography, 148–49
  data mining and metadata, 96, 99
  digital photographs, videos on, as
    unstructured data, 95–96

  structured data on images uploaded
    to, 96–97
SonicFinder, 228
Sony, 16, 115
Spacey, Kevin, 87–88
Stalin, Joseph, 126
Strava, 88–89
  global heatmap of, 88–89
  national security incident and,
    89–90, 100
Subtlety, A, or the Marvelous Sugar Baby
  (Walker), 132–34, *133*
Surrealism, 48
Surrey NanoSystems, 62
  Vantablack and, 62–65, *63*
surveillance, 101–9
  ACLU and civil liberty concerns, 103,
    109
  aerial reconnaissance airplanes, 106,
    107
  "aesthetics of surveillance," 103–4
  closed-circuit television cameras and,
    107
  drones and, 102, 103, 104–5
  IEDs and "Project Angelfire," 106–7
  Juarez, Mexico, and, 108
  moving backward and forward in
    time, 106–8, 109
  Paglen's photographs and, 101–2, *102*
  Strava's "heatmap," data on athletes
    and revealing military secrets,
    88–90
  Utah Data Center, 103–4
  warfare, combat, and, 104–7
  "wide field of view persistent
    surveillance (WFVPS) aerial
    collection asset," 106
systems, relevance of scale to, 19
  attunement to, awareness of, 214
  behaviors of, 19, 72, 74, 162, 179, 180,
    204, 211, 213
  biological, evolution and, 177–78,
    180

bottom-up (self-organizing or emergent) systems, 177–80, *181,* 188, 191, 193, 199, 222
bounded rationality and, 163
broken systems, 12–13, 136, 211
command-and-control mind-set for engineering, 213–14
complex systems, 205–12, 221–22, 231
description of, 211
example, toaster wiring diagram, 205
human and natural, interactions of, 211–12, 244n4
inflexible (example, tools), 176–77
leverage points for, 213
linear systems, 205
Monderman's traffic engineering and, 216–20, *217, 219*
as physical or immaterial, 204
planners, 209–10, 213
scaffolding and designing, 215–16
scalar framing and, 161, 163–64
scalar shifts or asymmetry and behavior change, 69–70, 72, 74, 162
scaling theory of change and, 202–3, 204
scaling up and, 203–4
social systems, 209, 211
technical, 212
top-down systems, 174–77, 180, *181,* 188, 191, 193, 197, 199, 221–22
what they are, 204
systems thinking, 4, 43, 205

TAI (International Atomic Time), 42
Tannenbaum, Andrew, 190
Taylor, Frederick W., 48
temperature, 2
decoupling from experience, 134
terabyte, 6
thermometers, 1, 2
This Is Spinal Tap (film), 23–24, *25*

time, 2
GMT and, 42
"leap second," 42–43
rotation of the earth and, 42
standard measurement (the second), 31, 41–42
Standard Time, 43
surveillance systems and moving backward and forward in time, 106–8, 109
System Time, 43
TAI and, 42, 43
Terrestrial Time, 43
Universal Time, 43
UTC and, 42–43
Toccata for Toy Trains (film), 142
Torvalds, Linus, 190, 191, 193–94, 197–98, 199, 245n8
opening post of 1991, 191–92, 196
post of 1992 on control of content, 193–94
traffic engineering, 216–21, *217, 219, 221*
Monderman's "shared space" and, 218–19
traffic circle, Concord, N.H., 220, *221*
Tree, The painting (Martin), *57,* 57
Tufnel, Nigel, 23–24, 25

Uber, 97, 99
United States
automobile subsidizing and, 158–59
bicycling in, scalar framing and, 149–61
"big three" automakers, 159
cyberattacks against, 117–18
first law on measurement, 29
interstate train system (Amtrak), 159
public policy and, 159
short scale model for numbers, 124
as wealthiest country, 12
wild pigs in the rural Southwest, 206–7
Untitled (Reaper Drone) (Paglen), 101–2, *102*

U.S. Army
  policy on data privacy, 89
  Strava security incident and, 89–90,
    100
UTC (Coordinated Universal Time), 42

van Bruggen, Coosje, 54
van Rijmenam, Mark, 92
Vantablack, 62–65, *63*, 66
Varian, Hal, 91
Verville, Andrew, 246n12
violence, 101–22, *102*, *113*, *121*
  algorithmic forms of policing, 106,
    121, 121–22
  aproportionalities and, 80, 105
  asymmetrical conflict, 80, 105,
    109–10, 112, 116–17, 118
  cyberwarfare, 111–19
  DDoS cyberattack, 111–15
  Google's Digital Attack Map and,
    112–13, *113*, 117
  IEDs and "Project Angelfire," 106–7
  netwar, 106, 118–19
  New York Times article on
    cyberattacks, 117–18
  "phase change" and, 119
  quantifying experience and, 120
  surveillance and, 101–9, *102*
virtual, augmented, and mixed realities,
    18, 65–66, 229
"Vitruvian Man" (Leonardo), 35

Walker, Kara, 230
  *A Subtlety, or the Marvelous Sugar
    Baby*, 132–34, *133*
warfare, combat. *See* tiny violence
Webber, Melvin, 245–46n9
  "Dilemmas in a General
    Theory of Planning," 208,
    210–11
Weber, Steven, 92–93
Weiss, Martha, 73
Went, Frits
  "The Size of Man," 70
  thought experiment, "Can an ant
    learn to read?," 70–72
West, Geoffrey, 238n16
White, John Myles, 91
wicked problems, 208–9, 212
Wikipedia, 83–84, 199, 240n13
  scale and, 84
Wilson, Mark, 229
Wired magazine, 190, 242n2
Wittgenstein, Ludwig
  Philosophical Investigations, 28–29
World in the Balance, The (Crease), 32
Worldwatch Institute, 150

Yin, Zhang-Qi, 76
Yoon, Soyoung, 242n17

Zeno's paradox, 215
Zuckerberg, Mark, 12, 167, 211

About the Author

Jamer Hunt is the Vice Provost for Transdisciplinary Initiatives at The New School and was founding director of the graduate program of Transdisciplinary Design at Parsons School of Design. He co-founded DesignPhiladelphia, the country's largest design week, and has published over two dozen articles for platforms such as *Huffington Post*. Named by *Fast Company* on their list of the "Most Creative People," he uses his unique background to reveal new vantages on the present. Learn more at JamerHunt.com.